MEMORIES OF OLD DORKING

Edited
by
Margaret K. Kohler

With
Illustrations and an Index

KOHLER AND COOMBES
DORKING
1977

Charles Rose's Recollections of Old Dorking were first published as articles in the West Surrey Times during 1876 and 1877, and reissued in book form 1878.

John Attlee's Reminiscences of Old Dorking was first published as an article in the Dorking Advertiser of 23rd March, 1912 and republished in booklet form by A.W. and W. Eade in 1952.

William Dinnage's Recollections of Old Dorking were first published as articles in the Dorking Advertiser in the summer of 1963.

Now all reprinted 1977 by Kohler and Coombes, 12, Horsham Road, Dorking, RH4 2JL.

Editorial matter copyright Margaret K. Kohler 1977.

ISBN 0 903967 08 1

Printed and bound in Great Britain by
The Scolar Press Limited, 59-61 East Parade
Ilkley, Yorkshire

Acknowledgements

Chris Kohler and John Coombes would like to thank all those people who have given them so much help and encouragement with the making of this book, particularly:

John Attlee
Miss Y. Bateman
Mrs. E.P. Chapman
Bert Coombes
Mr. and Mrs. Donald Dinnage
The Dorking Advertiser
The Dorking Library
The Dorking Museum Committee
Mrs. Winnie Eade
Kimble Earl
Miss Fanny Franks
Mrs. Joyce Hillis
Mrs. Victoria Houghton
David Knight
John Mee
Miss Doris Mercer
Mrs. Greta Morley
Mr. and Mrs. David Pygott
Mrs. Helen Rivers
John Walker

INTRODUCTION

This book is about people. The three Dorking Chicks whose recollections are here reprinted did not write for the summer visitors. They have nothing to say of Dorking's scenic beauties, picturesque promenades, gentlemen's seats.

Dorking for them was the community into which they were born, among whose people they grew up, and in whose life they took their part. Each of them on looking back saw, especially, people: people born and living and working within Dorking; people who provided within the town for most of the community's needs; neighbours and fellow-tradesmen who knew each other intimately. And so we have vivid pictures of life in our town from about 1825 - when George IV was King - to Queen Victoria's Golden Jubilee Year of 1887.

Charles Rose the linendraper of South Street knew not only who lived here or worked there, but how they lived and worked, and enjoyed themselves. Turning his pages at random we find stories of coachmen and of carriers' wagons, of jokers at the Pound, of Benefit Clubs, of schoolboys' Christmas letters to their parents. And we can feel that he was there, or heard all about it soon afterwards.

John Attlee, who knew Charles Rose, was the substantial businessman with a shop in the High Street, his home on Rose Hill, and the old family corn-mill near Station Road. In 1912, when he was eighty-four, he gave to the Dorking Advertiser's reporter a run-through of the tradesmen and residents of High Street, South Street and West Street of some sixty or seventy years earlier, updating as he went along - an amazing feat of memory. In 1952 Mr. & Mrs. A.W. Eade of West Street republished Attlee's recollections as a booklet, supplying footnotes to assist identification, and these are now supplemented to help the readers of 1977.

William Dinnage is the only one who put himself into his picture. The son of a bootmaker living in Hampstead Road, this sharp-eyed boy wandered and observed in the southern end of Dorking, venturing further into the town as he grew older. He recalls his daisy-grubbing for the old ladies up the road, his terror of the horseman's shaggy dog, the sight of pauper children behind the railings of the Workhouse playground, the sound of Shearburn's whistle. Often he halted to watch the builders at work, for Dorking's population was then well on its way to ten thousand, from the four thousand of Charles Rose's boyhood. In old age he walked again on Tower Hill and recalled the gentry of his youth, some of them so deeply concerned to give hope and help and encouragement to others; we hear of Miss Cotton's crowded meetings in the room in Pledge's Yard, and young William was there, too.

Many Dorkinians today are not true Five-clawed 'Uns - born in Dorking - as these three were. So let us enjoy their memories and through them come to feel our common citizenship.

RECOLLECTIONS OF OLD DORKING

by
Charles Rose

KOHLER AND COOMBES
DORKING
1977

Charles Rose

Born 2nd February 1818, son of Thomas & Ann Rose, and baptised in the Independent Meeting in West Street. (now the United Reform Church)

Died 12th January 1879, aged 60.

The "Recollections of Old Dorking" were published in the West Surrey Times during 1876 and 1877, and re-issued in book form in 1878. Writing of forty to fifty years earlier, his 'formerly' would have ranged from around 1825 to 1840.

Charles Rose says nothing of his family, yet it may be significant that he begins his review of the town in West Street (p.11), recalling in detail incidents and features that a child might well have noticed. He was the son of Thomas Rose who had a confectioner's shop opposite the Old House at Home.

In 1845 he set up on his own as a linen-draper, in a shop in South Street opposite the foot of Butter Hill. By the time of the census of 1871 Charles Rose was fifty-three, a widower with daughters of eighteen and sixteen, three employees in the business, a housekeeper and a domestic servant - all living over the shop. Next-door was a grocer, and on the other side an old-established firm of architects.

Charles Rose died in January 1879. Our only glimpse into his character comes in the kindly provisions of his will. He hoped that the business would be continued by his executors for the benefit of his dear daughter, Annie Tranter Rose, his only surviving child.. and that his executors would employ his trusty and valued assistant Mary Burden in its management..... and would recognise her long and faithful services to him especially in the remuneration which might be paid to her... One of the witnesses to the will was John Attlee.

The executors did continue the business, and then followed a Mr. Hicks and a Mr. Newitt. In 1906 Charles Degenhardt, newly married,

took over the succession; beginning with a
Sale he built up the business and eventually
expanded into the adjoining premises.
Architects are still next-door on the other
side.

RECOLLECTIONS

OF

OLD DORKING.

By Charles Rose.

Reprinted from the "West Surrey Times."

GUILDFORD:
PRINTED AT THE "WEST SURREY TIMES" OFFICE, HIGH STREET.

PREFACE.

THE "Recollections of Old Dorking," given in the following pages, refer chiefly to the state of things and events of from forty to fifty years ago. The greater portion of these reminiscences first appeared in the *West Surrey Times* during the years 1876 and 1877. At the close of their publication, many requests were made that they might be issued in a more permanent form. The wishes thus expressed are now complied with. The original subject-matter has been revised and new added, which, it is hoped, may prove acceptable; the original chronology, however, remains, for obvious reasons, unaltered.

All that is claimed for these "Recollections" is, that they describe in homely style, with an aim to be accurate, the state of the old town as it was, and the inhabitants as they were at the period referred to. It would be ungrateful on the part of the writer, were he not, before concluding this brief introduction, to acknowledge the much-valued aid of several kind friends, whose contributions and suggestions have materially added to whatever interest these "Recollections" may be thought to possess.

DORKING, April, 1878.

RECOLLECTIONS OF OLD DORKING.

A WALK THROUGH THE STREETS ON A SUMMER'S DAY HALF-A-CENTURY AGO.

The Dorking of fifty years ago was different in many respects from the Dorking of to-day. I intend to give my recollections of it in detail, as it then was. Let us first, however, get a glimpse of the old town by an imaginary walk through its streets. We enter the place by the London Road, say on a summer's morning half a century ago. Although yet early, the mill by the roadside is already at work, and the forge of the blacksmith's shop at the Reigate Road corner is in full blast. We pass along by the southern entrance of the neighbouring nursery grounds and see, just within their precincts, a board with the inscription, "Donald and Westland, nurserymen." The chestnut trees hard by, the broad green meadow, the mill-pond, and the distant hill are each of them objects of beauty. On the left hand is an antiquated-looking brick mansion, owned and occupied by a noble lady. The rooks in the rookery close by are uttering their morning caw, and the painted yeoman on the adjacent signboard is raising his sword in defiance of all invaders. It is only a little past six, yet many of the shops are already open, for the trading inhabitants of half a century ago were early risers, although by no means early closers. Tradesmen then had faith in long days of business, and took commercial matters in general more quietly and less hastily than in later days of restless and fierce competition. The mechanic in flannel jacket, cloth or paper cap and white apron, and the labourer in fustian or smock frock and straw hat, are already busily engaged at their callings. Sundry and divers poor people, with pitchers and cans in hand, are passing along to the dairies of the neighbouring mansions for a gratuitous supply of milk, the kindly custom of thus aiding the needy being then by no means an uncommon one. While passing along East Street we observe in the road a little man of about four feet nine gathering up dressing for his garden, and who used to say facetiously of himself that he grew but little till he was fourteen, and that then he made a surprising shoot! We reach the brow of the hill, and see on the right hand the word "Bank" stuccoed in front of a house, while on either side of the street are bow windows with small panes of glass. These, in fact, are the fronts of the grandest shops in the place, for plate-glass windows, with panes of gigantic size, were reserved for a later day for country towns like Dorking. On the left hand side of the street is the pebbled slope, where, on a Sunday morning, years before, had breakfasted some of the troops that were to escort, on the following day, Sir Francis Burdett to the Tower, and at which time, on being ordered to London for the same service, some of the Dorking Yeomanry Cavalry Corps it was said, fearful of consequences, made their wills. We now stroll up South Street, and reach the foot of Butter Hill, where, in front of one of the largest grocery establishments of the town, we observe at the edge of the pavement a row of primly trimmed elms, across the road the stocks, and a little higher up the street the pound for vagrant cattle. We pass the poplar and firs skirting the grass plat on the left, and reach another row of trimmed trees, this time of limes, in front of a private residence. We arrive soon after this, opposite the old Workhouse, the home for the poor. Here, too, close by, is the "Cage," the place of detention for persons no better than they ought to be. All along the route in South Street we see the footpaths, either unpaved, or "pitched," as in other parts of the town, with small oblong black sand stones. We reach the Queen's Head Inn, opposite to which, instead of a carriage entrance to a gentleman's mansion, there then stood a grocer's, baker's, and pork butcher's shop. We return now towards the centre of the town, and on the way see the milkmaid with dark lilac dress, cottage-shape straw bonnet, and snowy white apron. Now and then, we meet, too, an ancient dame, with a navy blue and white cotton gown, a yellow neckerchief, and a head gear to match in antiqueness. Early though it be, we observe here and there little boys at their morning game, dressed in the fashion of the day—a brown Holland pinafore, a frill round the neck, and a cloth cap of the old shape then worn. We approach the Bull's Head Inn, and see, as we near it, a coach with four splendid greys stands at the door. Some of the passengers have already taken their seats, and, like Englishmen, at all times, and at all seasons, are chatting with each other about the weather. A fine-built elderly man, with flowing coat, long gaping waistcoat, knee breeches, and buckled shoes, stands eyeing and admiring the beautiful creatures before him. This is one of the veterinary surgeons of the place, known by everybody as "Lord" Finch, who has come to see the start, before calling at the grocer's in West Street for his rasher for breakfast. Broad, the genial coachman, now appears at the inn door, and at this signal all the unseated passengers at once take their places. The church clock strikes seven, the familiar "Hold hard!" is heard, Lindsey, the ostler, snatches off the cloths, the greys prance impatiently, and off they go, first slowly, and then at a slapping pace, through the town towards the big City, to return again in the evening punctually at seven.

After breakfast, still on a summer's day, let us take another walk through the streets. We this time see a strong-built cart drawn by an equally strong horse, and with one or two attendants delivering to the various trading establishments the goods brought down the night before by the carrier's waggon, the then sole conveyance for heavy merchandize, for goods-trains and railway-vans in Dorking were at that time things to come. A lame-handed man, in ordinary clothes, and with a bag at his side, now emerges from a chemist's establishment in the High Street. He enters one shop and then another, stopping a short time at each. This is Postman Beadle, who is now making the one daily delivery for the town, and who stops to receive for each letter from London the high-priced fee of sixpence—a penny postage, and pre-payment by stamps, like thrice a-day deliveries in Dorking, being then boons of the "good time coming." As the morning passes we hear a number of cries in the streets: there is the vendor of vegetables from the parish garden, who announces somewhat timidly "all ware new potatoes;" the lame greengrocer from Epsom amplifies the cry by adding to the "all ware" the various vegetables in his cart; while his jocular competitor from Leatherhead, not to be outdone by either, shouts out more vigorously than truthfully, "Here's your sort, new potatoes, butter in 'em." At mid-day, up from West Street and bound for London, comes the carrier's waggon, laden toweringly high with unbent hoops; coach after coach, heavily weighted with passengers and luggage, now passes up and down, the metropolis and sea-coastwise. At a rattling pace, too, comes along a carriage and four, driven by postillions in gay attire; it slackens speed, and stops at the Red Lion Hotel. The occupants of the vehicle are a nobleman, or gentleman, and his family, who are posting, in the absence of express trains and first-class carriages, from the country or seaside seat to London. The equipage has hardly left the town when another and less pretentious vehicle approaches from the opposite direction, and pulls up at the inn a little lower down. This is our old familiar friend, the post-chaise, displaced in later days by vehicles of a modern shape and lighter construction. The postboy in charge is from the neighbouring town of Epsom, who, with short-knotted whip in hand, is dressed in the costume of his order—red jacket, white breeches, top boots, and the proverbial white hat. Warm is the reception given to him by his old acquaintances at the White Horse in blue, red, and yellow, one of whom, " the first turn-out," now takes his place and goes on to Horsham. Late in the afternoon a middle-aged man in high water-tight boots approaches the brow of the hill. The lad who attends him, one of his sons, strips off his shoes and hose, and forthwith the senior lays down by the side of the road and carefully adjusts a piece of wood with sacking attached. This is done to dam up the water, which is now turned on from the main, and the bay being well filled, the operation of watering the streets with a scoop is at once commenced. The church clock cherrily chimes the old 104th Psalm tune, and loudly strikes six. The evening coaches, one after another, now come in, and the huge lime-waggon is off to London. The familiar cry, " Salmon, salmon, fine pickled salmon !" in a fine bell-like tone, now arrests the ear, and many a supper-table, in those day of cheap fish, is all the richer for its being uttered. As the shades of evening come on there may be seen one after another of the older inhabitants leaning on the lower part of the street door —for doors then were not unfrequently divided into two— smoking his long clay pipe and chatting cozily with a neighbour, or saluting with a friendly "good-night" an acquaintance passing by.

A WALK THROUGH THE TOWN ON A WINTER'S DAY.

LET us pay another imaginary visit to the town half-a-century ago; this time on a winter's day. We see in the streets elderly matrons with scarlet cloaks, large black bonnets lined with white, and large bordered caps extending to below the chin. There are maidens also attired in short waisted dresses, beaver bonnets, and cloaks of a similar shape to those of their seniors. The men we meet too are dressed in clothes of an old-fashioned cut. Thus among the elders of the middle-class are to be seen ancient great coats, knee breeches, and top boots; among the juniors and middle-aged of the same class, pigeon-tailed, broad-collared, gilt-buttoned dress coats, and frilled shirt fronts; while among the sturdy sons of toil, dark round frocks, rough beaver hats and high leather-leggings are the general favourites. Let us gratify our curiosity by learning the price of provisions. We enter a grocer's shop and find the rates of foreign produce to be very high. Tea, a mixture of Congou and Twankay, the quality generally drunk, is 8s. the pound. The best kinds of tea, gunpowder and Pekoe, are from 12s. to 15s.; moist sugar in ordinary use is 8d.; lump ditto 1s., best loaf 1s. 2d. Currants are 1s. per pound, Valentia raisins 8d. Home produce we find is cheap. Best salt butter, Carlow or Waterford, is 11d.; fresh butter (it being winter) is 1s. 2d., in the summer it is 11d. Prime bacon 7½d. Derby and double Gloucester cheese 8d.; and Cheshire ditto 9d. per pound. Salt, chiefly in consequence of the duty, is 5½d. per pound. We find at the butcher's that prime joints of beef are 8½d. per pound, ditto of mutton 7d The pork butcher is selling fresh pork, legs, spareribs, and griskins, at 6½d., while those with little cash—from the low rate of wages and the number of mouths to feed—can buy the " hands " at 5d. per pound.

The afternoon arrives, and we hear the cheery cry of " Master " Woodger, the muffin and crumpet vendor, the stall keeper and delighter of the juveniles at Dorking and Punchbowl fairs—" Muffins O !" " Crumpets O !" " Muffins O !" " Crumpets too !" The shades of evening are coming on and we peer into the doorway of one of the smaller shops. The proprietor is stooping intently and patiently over a little round box on the counter before him. He is obtaining a light with flint and steel, tinder and brimstone match, for the more convenient and quickly lighting lucifer was not then invented. He now lights here and there a candle, and thus poorly illuminated the little establishment is kept open till nine, or it may be till ten o'clock. The larger establishments are better lighted; not, however, by gas, for which Dorking had to wait a little while longer, but by the old lamp then in vogue. We now see in the distance a wooden-legged man hasting along, and at his heels and on either side are a number of small boys.

He approaches, torch in hand, and with ladder on his shoulder, the nearest lamp in his way. This is lamplighter Wicks, who during the day has trimmed and stocked with oil the lamp he has now come to light. He climbs the ladder with marvellous rapidity, and, the work of lighting over, descends with a slide, and then amid a shout of the juveniles starts off to the next lamp, cracking jokes with the boys, and now and then saluting them with a blow of his wooden leg. The ringers, in the course of the evening, are at their wonted practice, and the bells give forth a merry peal. Otherwise, however, there is but little to interest, and but little to cheer in the dimly-lighted streets. The hours pass on, and nine o'clock arrives. Soon after this the mail cart stops at the Post-office, opposite the Wheatsheaf Inn. The mailman, well coated and muffled, at once withdraws his horse pistols from the holsters, proves to the acting official that they are duly loaded, and returns to the cart to place them whence they were taken. He now waits outside for the mail bags, and while doing so sundry and divers movements are afoot, indicating to the passer-by that the mailman is a penny the richer for a too late, yet important letter. The sealing of the bags is at length completed, and they are now deposited in the cart in safety. This accomplished, the mailman is quickly seated on his narrow box, and off he starts for Kingston, to return in the small hours of the morning. Such in mere outline were the appearance, life, and usages of old Dorking, about which, hereafter, I shall speak more particularly. In some respects, at least, its present inhabitants have but little cause to wish for a return of the "good old times."

THE OUTSKIRTS AND ENTRANCES OF THE TOWN HALF A CENTURY AGO.

WITHIN the last fifty years Dorking has grown considerably in size and doubled in population. At the census of 1821 the population of the parish was 3,812; in 1871 it was 8,567. Half a century ago the town was almost entirely comprehended in High Street, South Street, West Street, Back Lane, Mill Lane, and Ram Alley. True there were the outskirts also, including London Road, Cotmandene, and Spring Gardens, and these contributed their little quota of inhabitants. Let us glance round the town at the period referred to. Rose

Hill was then a park without a single residence, save that of its proprietor, upon it. The sites of Howard Road, Arundel Road, and Vincent's Road, were at that time meadows known as the Cat's Fields. The adjoining Vincent's Lane was then, on a summer's day, one of the prettiest shady retreats, resounding with the song of birds, and its banks bespangled with flowers, that town or village could boast of. Sandy Cross Lane—in a line with Vincent's to the southward—vied with it in its rural aspect and beauty. The thoroughfare now known as Hampstead Road was then a pretty country lane, where violets, celandine, and honeysuckle grew. Just at its termination in the Horsham Road were a blacksmith's shop on one side, and the Harrow toll gate and a cluster of fir trees on the other. Meadows and arable fields existed on the sites now comprehensively described as Falkland Road. The residence now called Barrington House, but then "The Orchard," the toll gate habitation, a cottage close by, a solitary dwelling at the entrance of Harrow Road east, and the Holloway farmhouse, comprised the whole of the residences in the Horsham Road, from the Queen's Head to the Hollow. To Harrow Road east, Tower Hill and the adjacent land, now studded with villas, bricks and mortar were then unknown. The whole of the Tower Hill district was, in fact, the home of hares, rabbits, and pheasants rather than of man. In this vicinity, it is true, there was, in years gone by, a human haunt, for hereabouts once stood a barn where the smugglers of the day, till informed against by one of their number, hid under its false floor their kegs of contraband spirits. Half a century ago the tower on the hill, and from which the latter derives its name, was not then erected. The site of the Union House was at that time an arable field, and the road now called St. Paul's, was then a quiet retreat, known familiarly, not only to lovers, many of whom have wooed or been wooed here, but to the inhabitants in general, as Sweetheart's Lane. Fewer changes have occurred in the northern and eastern outskirts of the town. Here, however, the railways and their stations, constructed during the last thirty years, have changed the aspect of the neighbourhood, and a considerable addition to the villa and other residences in the outskirts referred to, has since been made. Among the entrances to the town the greatest change has been made in the southern. This was partly effected some forty years ago, when the Hollow Hill was lowered, and the road raised from the foot of the hill to the Queen's Head Inn. Previous to this, the site of the present raised pathway was a part of the bank, which then sloped to the road. Along this bank grew a number of elm and holly trees, and, on the left of the road, a row of firs. The removal of these trees, of the old turnpike gate, and of the blacksmith's shop close by it, the construction of the pathway referred to, and the erection of the numerous residences which now fringe the roadway, have, of course, materially altered this entrance to the town. The western entrance, if we except the change at the lower end of Vincent's Lane, and the recent levelling of the sand rock opposite the Vicarage, presents but little alteration to the appearance of fifty years ago. The London Road entrance is but little altered, its principal changes being the erection of the immensely high wall on the left hand, the building of a boundary wall to the nursery grounds, and an improvement in some of the residences. In the Reigate Road entrance there have been greater changes. The old Punch Bowl, save the throwing open of its approach, is not a whit altered. The cemetery and the erections at its entrances are comparatively new. Nearer the town, the old Deepdene and Pipp Brook House Lodges have given place to new ones. The Deepdene coach road now stretches, as it did not then, across Fosterwoods Meadow; and the pathway, in bygone years, running from the old stile, which then stood at its south-western corner, is now diverted eastward. In addition to these alterations, there is the improvement in the highway, recently completed, and the disappearance of the old elm trees, and their saplings on the left of the road. Notwithstanding all the changes we have noticed, both here and at the other entrances and outskirts of the town, there are still unremoved landmarks, by which a long-absent native would be quick to recognise the well-known spots of his earlier days.

THE GENTLEMEN'S SEATS IN AND AROUND THE TOWN.

Half a century has wrought a complete change in the proprietorship and occupancy of the gentlemen's seats around Dorking. Denbies, at the commencement of that period was owned and occupied by William Joseph Denison, Esq., for many years one of the representatives of the county, and, from the passing of the Reform Bill till his decease, of the Western Division of Surrey. Mr. Denison was deservedly popular in Dorking, as a member of Parliament, a landed proprietor, and a neighbour. His services were always at the disposal of the inhabitants, whether in the franking of letters—a valuable privilege in high postage times—or in other matters. He gave also a willing support to objects designed to promote the welfare of the town, while his liberality in allowing a free access to his grounds was much appreciated. The hill in Mr. Denison's time, and I believe in that of his father also, was familiarly known among the inhabitants as " Denison's Hill." While referring to the elder Mr. Denison, it may not be uninteresting to narrate one or two incidents in his history. I remember hearing in bygone years, how in homely fashion, descending by the pathway which then ran down the ravine in front of the mansion, he would pay his visits to the town. Here in West Street dwelt an intimate friend of his, with the Christian name of Michael, who used to be saluted by the rich man of the hill as "Mike." The West Street resident inquiring on one occasion after the welfare of his companion, received, it is said, the facetious rejoinder, "Thank you, Mike, I can hardly keep the wolf from the door!" It is said that the elder Mr. Denison on his visits to the town would purchase and carry home a leg of mutton. This was done, it appears, from a grateful remembrance of the days when wealth had not poured its treasures into his lap. For it is said of him that when as a lad, anything but rich, he came from the North to London, his first day's dinner was from the remains of a joint of the kind referred to. Unlike many who have risen from poverty to wealth, he seems never to have wished to conceal his humble origin, but rather cherished the memory of it, by having in his later years a leg of mutton every day upon his table.

The Denbies Mansion of fifty years ago was by no means a fine one, either in regard to its size, elevation, or the style of its architecture. The old building on the purchase of the estate by the late Thomas Cubitt, Esq., father of the present senior member for West Surrey, soon gave place to the present magnificent one erected on its site.

The Deepdene half a century ago was in the possession and occupation of Thomas Hope, Esq., who greatly enriched its artistic and other treasures, and to him succeeded, a few years later, his son, the late Henry Thomas Hope, Esq., who made extensive improvements in the mansion.

Betchworth Castle, now a decaying ivy clad ruin, was fifty years since the seat of Henry Peters, Esq., and was subsequently and finally the residence of David Barclay, Esq. On the vacation of the castle by Mr. Barclay, its dismantlement was proceeded with, and the remains of this fine old residence, once the busy scene of human life, became silent and solitary, the haunt of owls, and the nesting place of other birds. This third demolition of a mansion on the Deepdene estate—one having once stood in Chart Park, and another on the site of the present Deepdene Gardens—produced, as in the two previous instances, much regret among the inhabitants.

The possessor and occupier of Bury Hill fifty years ago was Robert Barclay, Esq., a great grandson of the renowned apologist of the same name, and the great grandfather and namesake of its present proprietor. Mr. Barclay, as is well known, once belonged to the Society of Friends, from which, on his marriage, however, he became disconnected. Notwithstanding this separation he ever afterwards cherished a high esteem for the religious body he had left, and emulated it in the cause of education, and in acts of benevolence. He founded and supported the school, conducted for many years in Hampstead Lane, and so apostolically bishop-like was he as "a lover of hospitality," and "a lover of good men," that he used to invite to the same table the Vicar of the parish, and the Independent Minister, and was accustomed to send his carriage to convey them in the company of each other to his mansion. Well would it be were a similar liberality more generally exhibited in the present day. On the decease of Mr. Barclay, Bury Hill was inherited by his son, Mr. Charles Barclay, by whom the mansion was greatly improved.

The proprietor of Pipp Brook Mansion at the same period was William Crawford, Esq., M.P. for the City of London, and the able and active Chairman of the Dorking Bench of Magistrates. His son, Mr. R. W. Crawford, who succeeded his father in the representation of the City, afterwards occupied the old mansion. This, in every respect, was far inferior to the existing one, erected a few years ago, by the late Mr. Foreman.

Shrub Hill, fifty years ago, was owned and occupied by the Countess of Rothes, relict of the Earl of Rothes, Colonel of the Surrey Yeomanry Cavalry. Here resided also the Lady Mary Leslie and the Lady Elizabeth Leslie, the daughters of the Earl. Shrub Hill Mansion still retains the exterior characteristics it had at the time referred to.

Sondes Place, or, as it was then commonly called, Sand Place, now the Vicarage, was at the same period occupied by Hugh Bishop, Esq., and about forty years ago by Mrs. Barclay, relict of Mr. Robert Barclay. The principal alterations which have been made in the old residence from the time Mr. Bishop occupied it, are a new wing on the western side, the added approach on its eastern, and the closing of the old carriage entrance in the Westcott Road.

Rose Hill was, fifty years ago, the property of Richard Lowndes, Esq., who then occupied its only mansion—a residence where Louis Phillipe, the King of the French, spent some of his childhood in the stormy days of the first French Revolution. It is interesting to know that when the ex-King, a few years before his death, alighted at the South-Eastern Dorking Station, he inquired after the residence where, in his early years, he found a refuge. It so happened, however, that no one then at the station knew where it was, or it is probable that the aged monarch would have looked once again upon a spot that he had well-known ere so chequered a history had befallen him. Half a century ago the archway, now a public entrance to Rose Hill, was the rear approach to the mansion, then rendered private by gates a little nearer the street. The course of the public footpath, running from east to west on the brow of the hill was, it is said, some seventy years ago more northerly. The outskirts through which the footpath passes were, fifty years ago, generally known as the "Back Fields." Although, as already stated, Rose Hill is so different from what it once was, its ancient mansion is all but unchanged.

A GENERAL REVIEW OF THE TOWN.

West Street.—North Street.—Back Lane.—A Broad Hint.—A Well-known Character.—Relics of the Old Queen's Arms.—The Old King's Head.—Two Irish Wakes.—The Old Rectory.—A Gang of Highwaymen.

Let us now review in detail the interior of the town at the period referred to. We will enter the place, this time at its west end. The changes just at the entrance have been already noticed. We pass them by, therefore, and arrive at the lower end of West Street. We see here, on the left hand, the old barn where, in the autumn, the produce of the "Popper," or "Pupper" (after it ceased to be a furze field) was garnered, and where, in the winter, the stroke of the thresher's flail resounded. Here, too, in the same farm-yard was a thatched-roofed shed, where, in days that are past, the sound of milking and the song or the whistle of the milker might be heard. A little to the eastward, on the same side of the road, is an old brick-house, with a wheelwright's shop, or what was formerly so, attached. Here lived, fifty years ago, an enterprising tradesman, who was at that time part proprietor of one of the old coaches, and who was carrying on business also as a farmer, a wheelwright, and a timber merchant, supplying at times timber for the Royal Navy. "Neighbour" Chitty, the tradesman referred to, lived to the great age of about ninety, and for many years he might be seen on a summer's evening reclining against the post in front of his residence. Close by the wheelwright's shop, I have heard, there stood, sixty or seventy years ago, an elm tree of extraordinary size. Vincent's Walk, on the opposite side of the road, was, at one time called Cat's Fields Alley, and had, till a comparatively recent period, a deep ditch on its left hand side. A little further up the street, on the site of the mason's yard, adjoining Clarendon House, then Grove House, was the stabling establishment, where, forty years or more ago, flys were first started in Dorking, of which it was predicted, at the time, that "they might live in the summer, but they would die in the winter." On the rear portion of the site, where the Star now stands, was, in bygone years, an old blacksmith's shop. The front part of the site was occupied by an old sweet shop, a favourite resort for the boys and girls of fifty years ago for delicious lollipops and bonny brown-striped bullseyes! Just outside the shop door was a large boulder, placed here to guard the footpath and the entrance to the drain, which, although the drainage of the town was then generally above ground, was here rendered necessary, by the roadway intercepting the water-course. The Parsonage, now known as Parsonage House, was occupied fifty years ago by the portly Mr. Greaves, a well-known miller and agriculturist. The old residence, in his time, and indeed till very recently, had a plain brick exterior, over which grew a luxuriant pear tree. We miss the old green gate at the entrance to the yard, and the elm tree close by, where the blacksmiths, from the neighbouring smithy, bent their wheel tires. The old limes and the laburnum in front of the house are also gone. The lower part of the premises, in which the candle factory and wholesale grocery establishment now stand, was a farm-yard, where, about forty years ago, an incendiary fire of a most alarming nature occurred. On the left hand side of the entrance to the Washway, now the Station Road, was a deep ditch, along which flowed the surface and domestic waste water from the western and southern parts of the town. Sewage, in the present acceptation of the term, there was none. The Washway, or Pipp Brook, unlike its now polluted condition, was then a clear stream, on the bed of which its weeds and fishes might be plainly seen. The Washway bridge of half-a-century ago gave place some years since to the present wider, and, in other respects, improved structure. The old erection, it appears, was not of long duration, for an aged inhabitant has told me that sixty years or more ago a still older bridge, composed simply of one or two planks and a hand-rail, spanned the brook. Before leaving this spot, we note the change which the railway has brought. The old mill on the stream, however, is yet going, and the adjacent works, which were erected about forty years ago, still manufacture the illuminating gas. On our way back to the town we no longer see the high whitethorn hedge protecting the orchard on the left, or the meadows on the right without a habitation upon them. The old Spring Gardens are all but unchanged. There is now, as there was then, and, perhaps, had been a century or two before, the old cottage close by their entrance, with the spring (which in all probability gave its name to the gardens) still issuing so strangely beneath it. Fifty years ago there was yet another spring, with water as clear and pure, a few yards lower down. This, however, was utilised some time ago in augmenting the Waterworks supply. Nearer the bridge, too, was a cluster of minor springs; for the spring stratum being here so near the surface, little boys, in times gone by, amused themselves by making springs.

Let us now return to West Street. Here, on the site of the Public Hall, stood, half-a-century ago, the chief boys' school of the place, in front of which were two or three fir trees. Against the wall in front of the Academy was an old toll bar, which, when closed, stretched across the road to a post near the boulder opposite. It is said that the toll was an Excise one, and that the amount levied was $2\frac{1}{2}$d. on each taxed vehicle. The old bar still remained long after the toll had ceased to be demanded. Close to the Academy was a plumber and painter's shop, where for a series of years the Shrove Tuesday footballs were gratuitously painted. Directly opposite, forty years ago, the first iron foundry in Dorking was opened. The two old-fashioned houses on the right were not then transformed into "The Old House at Home." Near here, but a short distance from the street, there still stands the old residence where then lived an excellent Christian man, bowed down with age, and very deaf, who, in his younger days, was coachman to the venerated John Wesley. Here, too, lived a relative of the worthy old man who less abstemious than he, had a craving for ale. This not unfrequently led the relative referred to to ask his good mother's customers, much to her annoyance, for his favourite beverage. Though not intellectually brilliant, poor fellow, the following incident will show that our thirsty friend was not a little 'cute in endeavouring to gratify his inclination, in this instance I believe with success:—One day, having received a commission to deliver half-a-sack of flour to Mr. M——, a bootmaker, in High Street, he was thus admonished: —"You are to take this flour to Mr. M——, and mind you don't ask him for beer, but if he offers you any you may have it." The flour was duly delivered, and with it this extremely broad hint:—"If you please, Mr. M——, I have brought your flour, and mother said I wasn't to ax you for any beer, but if you offered me some I might have it!"

As we pass up the street we miss, close by the entrance to Junction Road, an old barn, a part of which was used fifty years ago as stabling. The street exterior of this building was then utilised as a bill-posting station, and on it at the period referred to were the huge flaming posters announcing those tempting ventures of the day—the lotteries. The lower end of the Junction Road was then part of a carrier's yard, in which were a brewery, a slaughter-house, and extensive storage for unbent cask hoops and for merchandise in general. In this capacious yard, early in the year 1828, a large concourse of people assembled from the neighbourhood and from places miles around, to celebrate the very remarkable success of the late Mr. Thomas Rose, in the treatment of hundreds of cases of small-pox. The proceedings were enlivened by the Dorking Band, and headed by this a procession of those present afterwards paraded the streets of the town.

The grocery establishment, or rather the house in which the business is carried on, nearly opposite the yard, has an interesting association connected with its history. An old deed engrossed in antique style, states that this " messuage or tenement" was given in "the ffiue and twentieth year of the reigne of our Sovereign Lord, Charles II. . . . . Anno Dom., 1673," by one Martha Hall, "to her sonn William, for and in consideration of the naturall loue and affection she bore unto her said sonn, and for other good and sufficient causes and valuable considerations." The town, in this old parchment, is called "the towne of Dorking," thus bearing testimony, as we believe other and older documents do, to the fact that the present name of the place is the ancient one, and that the designation of "Darking," by which the town was very generally known at the beginning of the present century, was a corruption of the original name. Various improvements have been made in the shops and residences in this part of West Street; there is but little change, however, in the venerable and homely King's Arms, whose present hostess bears the same surname as that of the landlord of half a century ago. There is still the tablet on the house opposite, although now almost obliterated by paint, announcing, as it did then, that William Williams gave this tenement, the adjoining one, and certain lands, including the old carrier's yard referred to, and a plot of ground near Denbies, to the parish of St. Andrew, Holborn, for ever. By virtue of which gift the incumbent and parochial officers of the said parish, as custodians of the property, now and then visited Dorking to view and take action respecting it. Close by the Plat to the eastward, still stands an old erection, in which were made in large mash tubs, more than 500 plum puddings, for the Reform Dinner on Cotmandene. The old residence at the lower end of the enclosure has the same familiar frontage now as it had then. We now come to the builder's yard on the opposite side of the street—a yard suggestive of the mutations of human life, and of waggons laden with lime, used in bygone days in erecting "new" London Bridge, the Houses of Parliament and other great and important public works. The old Meeting House, or Chapel, then standing, like its successor, on the left hand, and the Quakers' or Friends' Meeting House on the right, still further up the street, I intend to notice in a future chapter or two devoted specially to the old places of worship. The Rose and Crown presents pretty much the same appearance as it did fifty years ago. Not so, however, the Bell, then known as the Star, for this has undergone considerable alteration since worthy Host Potter in his old-fashioned smock frock was its landlord, althcugh happily the ancient brackets with the date 1591 inscribed on them still remain over the gateway. Many have been the changes in the old town since these antique relics were carved in the reign of Queen Bess. The very old houses probably of the same date as the old Star, and adjoining the latter to the eastward still stand, and if we except some alterations in the lower part of them, are almost unchanged from half a century ago. The new houses opposite to them occupy the site of what was then a grass plot in front of the Friends' old Meeting House, which ancient building still stands at the rear of these residences. A little higher up on the same side of the road stood anything but a superlatively respectable dwelling, used as a traveller's home, and popularly designated " The Beggar's Opera." This establishment was conducted, at the time referred to, by a witty and remarkably genial character known commonly as " Farmer George," who afterwards became a vendor of cakes and sweetmeats at fairs and clubs, and of periwinkles and mackerel in the streets. Of the last named he would shout, too frequently on a Sunday morning, " Here's your sea hogs." While of the periwinkles he would cry, regardless of correct pronunciation, but with a facetiousness and joviality perfectly natural to him " Peniwink, peniwink, peniwink, O ! Get a pin, stick him in, turn him round, pull him out, peniwink, wink, wink, wink, O !"

On the opposite side of the road, the old blacksmith's shop, with its roaring forge, its noisy anvil, and its shouting sons of Vulcan, has given place to a quieter and far more attractive establishment. Adjoining the smithy, towards the east, was the residence of its proprieror, one of whose sons was collector at the old toll-bar at the lower end of the street.

Happily the shoot-pipes, once projecting from the houses hereabouts, no longer pour down their contents, as in days of old, upon the drenched passers by.

At the top of the street a great change has taken place, for fifty years ago the site of the drapery and clothing establishment now erected here was a carrier's yard, approached by two old gates from the street. Within the yard was a curious gallery of carved woodwork, after the manner of the old hostelries. This unquestionably belonged to the Queen's Arms, which in all probability, one or two centuries ago, was the first and most extensive inn of the town. Tradition says, indeed, that, at one time, this old hostelry extended down the street as far as the Bell, and it is certainly a singular coincidence, if it be not corroborative of the tradition referred to, that the sign of the old inn bore the same date as that on the brackets over the Bell gateway. The fact is well authenticated that the Queen's Arms occupied the site of at least two of the houses at the top of the street. The style of its architecture was pure Elizabethan. This is shown by a pencil sketch which is still preserved. The arms on the signboard were those of Elizabeth.* An eye witness, born within the precincts of the old hostelry, states of the old signboard that she has often seen it, but a recent search failed to discover it, and there is too much reason to fear that it is now destroyed.

The relics of the old Queen's Arms that yet remained within the last half century were, on the testimony of the witness referred to, of a most interesting character. These ancient remains, besides the gallery already described, comprised the kitchen, bar, and ball-room of the inn. The kitchen was for many years before its demolition the dwelling place of a labouring man and his family. Of its capaciousness some idea may be formed when it is stated that it contained, while thus inhabited, two four-post bedsteads and a faggot stack! The fire place was utilised as the sitting-room of the family, and had within it a table and a number of chairs. Close by the kitchen was the bar, an oaken enclosure, resembling in appearance one of the very large and high old pews once existing in ancient churches. The ball-room of the inn was a perfect marvel, for around its walls, to the height of six or seven feet, was an elaborate needlework tapestry representing Pharaoh and his host in the Red Sea, while the space above the tapestry was covered with bronzed leather, embellished with gilding. The room had as its occupant, some years before its destruction, a person of miserly habits, and on his decease, so great was the desire to possess his accumulated hoard, that the tapestry, behind which it was supposed to be hidden, was ruthlessly pulled down and used as a carpet. This act of Vandalism had its reward in the discovery of a part of the supposed hidden treasure, and another portion of the hoard was found

---

* The following is the description of the old sign given in Brayley's "History of Surrey":—"It bears the arms of Queen Elizabeth—viz., France and England quarterly, encircled by the Garter, with the initials E. R. The supporters on the dexter side a lion ramp. guard-crowned Or, on the sinister a red dragon; above the latter is a white and red rose, and on the dexter a *Fleur-de-lis*, both ensigned with the Royal Crown. There is also the date 1591." . . . .

buried in a fireplace beneath the sweepings of years. In addition to the money deposited in the last-named place, there was discovered a Bible, the leaves of which, apparently where it had been read, were stuck over with hundreds of pins. One would have been glad to have hoped that, instead of burying the Holy Book with his hoard—probably from a lingering affection for a former owner—the miser had himself perused its pages, and found therein the true riches.

Let us now enter the thoroughfare known by various names, not the least appropriate of which is North Street. Here, on the right hand, we see, but little changed in half a century, the ancient buildings once forming part of the old King's Head. Of late years the ancient inn has had a memento in the revived "Old King's Head." It was here that the first of the two Irish "Wakes" held in Dorking within the memory of living inhabitants was held. One of the sons of Erin, who had been working at the Chalk Pit, met there a fatal accident. The means, it appears, were not forthcoming to defray the expenses of the funeral, and an application was made by some of his countrymen to a wealthy lady in the neighbourhood for assistance. The necessary amount was subscribed, but on the express condition that no rite of the kind alluded to should be observed. The "Wake," however, took place, and, to secure its secrecy, was held in the middle of the night. Immediately after this, it is stated, the participators in the "Wake," probably afraid of the discovery of their breach of good faith, left the town, and were not heard of from that time. The second "Wake" referred to will be described presently. The house opposite, known as the "Gun," is a very old one, and probably at one time was a rear portion of the Queen's Arms. The old King's Head Square is all but unchanged. Not so, however, the part of the lane, or street, lower down, for the tenements, with the gardens in front of them, were not there fifty years ago. Then, on the site of the malthouse, were cottages of puny size and height, in front of which might be seen an ancient dame smoking her evening pipe, and in whose honour, it is said, the bell of the old Market House had been rung on her wedding day. The opposite corner has been revolutionised, for instead of the present modern dwellings there was then, a few yards from the road, a very ancient erection, with an elder tree by its side, which at one time was the vicar's, or rather the rector's residence, and where, in all likelihood, dwelt the Rector of Dorking, who became a Nonconformist on the passing of the Act of Uniformity. This old dwelling was occupied for many years by Mr. J. Paul Cleere, the parish clerk. It is interesting to know that representations of this relic of the past have been carefully preserved. A little way down Back Lane, on the left hand, was a soap factory, where the laundresses of bygone years obtained lees for washing purposes. This factory was carried on for some time by Mr. William Moore, who succeeded his father-in-law, Mr. Walker, in whose family the soap-boiling business had been for two or three generations. Although fifty years ago there was no Wesleyan Chapel on the site of the present edifice, it is stated that the old building further down the lane, known as the Chapel Cottages, but formerly as the Barracks, was at one period a Wesleyan place of worship. It is said also that the founder of Wesleyan Methodism preached there. It is certain that a portion of the erection alluded to was, some sixty years ago, used for the purpose of preaching, for this fact has been certified by one of the hearers. Here it was that the second Irish " Wake," to which we have already referred, was held. This incident occurred about forty years ago, and the details of it, incredible and sickening though they are, are thus described by an eye-witness :—" The body of the deceased man was placed on a chair by the side of a table. Before it was a mug of beer. Around, and supplied with food and drink, were the poor fanatical people who had assembled to wake the departed out of his long deep sleep. One after another of those present then uttered the doleful cries, " O, Willie, why did ye die, and leave all these good things behind ye ?' ' O, Willie, why did ye go, and leave all these good things behind ye ?' It need hardly be said, however, that poor 'Willie,' notwithstanding these plaintive invocations and the shocking indignity to which his remains were subjected, still slept the sleep of death."

The old Waterworks, which were founded in the reign of George II., furnished to the inhabitants of fifty years ago a supply of pure water. Originally the service was through wooden pipes, the bursting of which (a by no means unfrequent occurrence) gave great delight to the youngsters. It must be forty years ago when I saw the last of these bored old tree trunks, decayed and sodden by leakage, give place to iron pipes. Church Street received its name on the erection of the modern-looking tenements on its left hand side, five or ten years before the last-named period. Before the erection of the dwellings referred to, there stood on the site of the more eastern of them an old barn, owned by the late Mrs. Harriott Cheesman, who kindly allowed the poor to thresh in it the leasing corn which they and their children had gathered. The house at the right hand of the street entrance was, years before, the residence of a plumber, who, it is said, on a high-bred horse, and in companionship with a doctor and lawyer in the town, and a farmer on the Holmwood, pursued, for miles round Dorking, the hazardous calling of a highwayman. In the time of these banditti the Hollow, south of the town, was a dreaded place of robbery, and it was here that the farmer highwayman and one of his fellow robbers were lurking one night for victims. The former, mistaking his companion for a different kind of game, demanded of the other his money. Instead of standing to deliver, however, the latter gruffly, but jocularly, retorted—"Dog eat dog! Don't you know me, T——?" A worse adventure, it is stated, happened afterwards to one of the highwaymen. During a marauding expedition—and, as it proved, his last— the robber referred to ventured as far as Wimbledon. Here, on the common, as the story goes, he met and stopped a gentleman of colour, who, instead of delivering his cash, fired at the robber his pistol. The last-named, though mortally wounded, was able to reach his home, where, shortly afterwards, he died. Rumour said he had succumbed to black fever, but the pipe-loving old dame already alluded to, and who performed the offices for the dead, used to say somewhat grimly that "it was not *black* but *lead* fever" that ended the robber's career.

A GENERAL REVIEW OF THE TOWN.

HIGH STREET, EAST STREET, COTMANDENE.—A FREAK WITH THE PERIWIGS.—THE OLD CHEQUERS.—DISSIPATED SOLDIERS.—IMPUDENT THIEVES.—DARING SMUGGLERS.— THE OLD MARKET HOUSE.—A MOUNTEBANK TRICK.

Let us now return to the western end of High Street. Here the town pump of half a century ago stood on the same site as the present one. How long the old one had existed I know not, though probably it was not here when bulls were baited at a bull ring, as it is said they were, close by, if not on this very spot. The baker's and confectioner's establishment at the rear of the pump was there fifty years ago, and had been, indeed, for almost the same period before that time, the date of its origin being 1779. Within a stone's throw of this spot, in fact, are to be found the largest number of the most ancient houses in the town. The old residence of Coachman Broad, whence, in bygone days, he emerged with punctuality in the morning to take charge of his favourite greys, still stands, looking, however, still more diminutive since the adjoining drapery and clothing establishment displaced the very old houses that stood on its site. It was only some forty years ago that the Post Office was removed to where it now is, for the little postal business of previous years was conducted at the establishment now known as the Medical Hall, Mr. H. Lanham, who had for some time efficiently managed the business of the office, thereupon becoming the postmaster. The ancient hostelry, the King's Head—a part of which is now occupied by the Post Office—must in its palmy days have been an extensive one. Many have been the occupants of the several portions of the old inn, and very varied its uses, since then. Close to the Post Office, and no doubt once belonging to the Inn, is the King's Head or Anchor Yard, the last-named appellation being, in all probability, derived from the brewery, now no longer in operation, within its precincts. Within the yard some five-and-forty or fifty years ago lived a barber who, by constitution and habits, was just the character to invite the attention of the practical jokers of the town, and this attention he certainly had. One night these wags of the period, bent upon fun and frolic, abstracted the barber's periwigs, and great was his trouble in consequence; the loss of an elderly maiden's white one giving him special concern. In the morning it was noised abroad that the wigs had been found, not, however, where the barber would have them—in his shop—but placed in a row on poles along the Church pavement. The actors in the affair were soon suspected, and summoned to the Bench. Finding their position a little too serious, they now attempted a compromise, and an offer of £5 was made accordingly to stay proceedings. But this was not all, for the barber had a wife, whose familiar name was "Sally." With a keen appreciation of human nature, and as a clever stroke of policy, the wags in trouble sought to bribe the barber's spouse. "Sally" was offered, in fact, the tempting prize of a new gown. Even this, however, was unsuccessful. The barber was inexorable, and before the Justices the culprits were brought. Information, it appears, was given to the noble Chairman of the Bench as to the proffered compromise, and, addressing the prosecutor, he inquired how it was that offers so liberal had not been accepted. Now our friend the barber was an enterprising man, who turned an honest penny by letting out a pony, and having lost this useful animal, he wished to supply its place. Using a common, but not elegant, phrase of his, he replied to the Bench with admirable candour—" Dang the little nation, I wanted to get another pony." The Bench, however, reproved the barber for his covetousness, and seeing at once that the case originated in a joke, thought the £5 offered an ample compensation, and thus was dissipated, no doubt to "Sally's" disappointment, the vision of the new gown. Whether a curtain lecture was delivered that night I never heard. Possibly there was. The jokers, it is certain, had to pay dearly for their whistle, or to be plain, for their freak with the periwigs.

Chequers Yard, or, as it is usually called, Chequer Yard, derived its name unquestionably from the ancient Inn which once existed at its High Street entrance. The house on the eastern side of the entrance, either constituted the old hostelry, or formed a part of it. I cannot state the exact time when the Chequers was closed, but that it existed late in the last century, or even early in the present one, is pretty certain, for an aged inhabitant well remembers an ostler of the old Inn. There appears to be good reason for believing, too, that a considerable business was done both here and at the two old hostelries almost opposite—the King's Head and the Queen's Arms—in the way of posting. It would be interesting to trace the causes which led to the rise of three such extensive Inns so near to each other, and equally interesting to know the circumstances that led to their decline. One thing is clear, that when travelling was slow, these old hostelries flourished, and when it became more rapid they declined. I have heard that one of them was shut up through its landlord closing his doors on the prospective arrival in the town of some hundreds of soldiers, which act of his forfeited his license, and rendered its obtainment thereafter impossible. It would appear from this, that the innkeepers of that period had reasons to complain, as those in the present day justly have, of an inadequate remuneration for the reception of the military. The loss which appeared in prospect, however, seems insufficient to account for the closing of the Inn, had it been in a state of prosperity. Apart from the question of remuneration the frequent removal of soldiers during the wars at the commencement of the century must have tried not a little the patience of Inn proprietors, for so great at that period was the pressure for accommodation, that not only the Inns of the town, but those of the villages around also, were at times brought under contribution. This was especially the case during the war of 1809, in which year a party of soldiers about to join the Walcheren Expedition was billeted at the Duke's Head, Bear Green. These poor fellows, who were just at the time flushed with bounty or prize money, yielded themselves up to the most lamentable dissipation and folly. Among the mad freaks they indulged in, were the frying of their watches, the tying round the necks of geese of one pound notes, and by way of variation in amusement, the eating of some of the latter between slices of bread and butter! It was by no means surprising that, with such a state of demoralisation, the baggage waggons should be laden with numbers of these erring men, nor if such were the condition of the troops generally, that the disastrous expedition referred to should have so signally failed.

At this same old Inn, too, though in later years, another incident equally memorable took place. The landlord of the house—Mr. Wood—had a brood of geese fattening for Michaelmas or Christmas. Some impudent rogues being aware of this fact coveted or, as they put it, wished to purchase the birds referred to, not, however, at a price mutually agreed upon, but at one fixed by themselves. No doubt anticipating the landlord's objection to their terms, they visited his premises in the dead of the night, and there and then transacted the business. Next morning the owner, innocent of what had happened, found that the female birds had disappeared, while around the neck of the male one was a paper containing a number of pence and having on it the following doggerel lines:—

> Mister Wood, your geese are good,
> And we are men from yander,
> We have bought your geese, at a penny a piece,
> And left the money with the gander.

To return, however, to the entrance of Chequer Yard. Here, in the windows of the grocery establishment on its eastern side, and in the window of the drapery establishment a little higher up the street, we have almost the only specimens of importance left of the bow shape, once all but general in principal shops of the town. Steps, too, like those at the entrance of the grocery establishment were at one time equally general. Opposite here the old malt-house and the ancient residence in front of it fifty years ago, have long given place to the grocery establishment now designated the "Golden Canister." The old Wheatsheaf Inn, if we except a slight improvement in the lower part of it, looks about the same as when the huge stuffed hog was exhibited here in years gone by. This prodigy of the porcine race, which had been bred on the premises, and for seeing which a charge of two-pence was made, was at the time one of the wonders of the place. The late Mr. John Timbs in his *Promenade Round Dorking* (written in 1822), says of this extraordinary animal, that "accidentally breaking one of its legs it was killed without fatting; its skin was dressed with the hair on, and is now preserved, stuffed, and standing in full proportion. It exceeded in size the famous Northumberland hog of the year 1543. It weighed 104 stone, or 832lbs. Its length, 12 feet; girth, 8 feet; height, 18 hands, and, it is computed, had it been fatted proportionably, it would have weighed nearly 200 stone!" From the Wheatsheaf to where the gifted writer alluded to then lived, is but a few steps, for it was at the chemist's establishment opposite that Mr. Timbs was apprenticed, and it was here that he penned his first literary production—the little work referred to. Few establishments in the place, perhaps, have seen greater changes, or have been more improved than this. An old inhabitant, for instance, remembers four successive alterations in the shop front, the first, which existed sixty or seventy years ago, being of a very primitive description. The window stall-board of the original front, he states, was so high as to permit a shutter suspended from hinges, to drop down below it, and this arrangement, he affirms, was then the usual one in regard to the shop fronts generally. This was confirmed by a still more aged resident, lately deceased, who distinctly remembered when the first bow shop window—at that time no doubt regarded as a grand affair—was put in.

The site of the London and County Bank was, half-a-century ago, that of one of the oldest watchmaker's shops in the town. Next to this was an equally old candle factory, which is now superseded by a manufactory of patent medicines, while the old shop in which the "dips" were hung aloft is now stocked with drugs, and so improved and embellished as to be quite unlike its former self. The wine and spirit establishment adjoining the Wheatsheaf was the site of one of the old private banks. Cape Place received its name fifty years ago from its owner, a successful colonist from the Cape of Good Hope.

On the south side of the street is a great improvement, for the old pebbled slope once extending from the pavement to the road was superseded some years ago by the present stone wall, thus giving a valuable addition of width both to the footpath and roadway. This much needed alteration was carried out chiefly through the late Mr. James White, to whom the town was indebted also for other important improvements.

The Church entrance, now generally called the Church Passage, was, in years gone by, known as the Church Gates, for at the street end of the footway there then stood two old wooden gates. These, however, were removed on the erection of the iron ones at the lower end of the passage. Close by the Church gates an ancient low built glass and china warehouse has given place to Auction and Estate Agency Offices with a commanding elevation. A little to the eastward, on the same side of the street, the lately re-erected ironmongery establishment now occupies the site of another of the old banks, and an office of a third bank is now absorbed in the drapery establishment almost directly opposite. The baker's shop which so long occupied the site of the jewellery and upholstery establishments close by has, with its old-fashioned bow window, now been gone for some years. Although all along the High Street time has brought its changes, in some instances by the substitution of a new house for an old one, and in more by giving an old friend a new face, its general aspect is that of a familiar acquaintance.

The Red Lion Hotel, with so many reminiscences of stirring events, where so many assemblages, magisterial and deliberative, grave and gay, have taken place, still stands. Here how often, when an alleged offender has been summoned, or in common parlance, "pulled up the steps," has the father or mother, or, it may be, the husband or the wife of the accused, waited in dreadful suspense the magistrates' decision. Here, too, the riotous mob has assembled, and the stirring scenes of a hotly-contested election, in the olden time, been witnessed. Scarcely less exciting was an incident which occurred here, when, in years gone by, bands of bold smugglers on swift horses, with kegs of spirits slung on either side of the saddle, travelled by the way of Dorking from the seacoast to London; when, too, along the route sympathising farmers found for them sham hay and corn ricks, in which to store temporarily the smugglers' ill-gotten booty. Apprised that a gang of these desperadoes was about to pass through the town, the Excise officers of the period sought the aid of the military to arrest them. A squad of soldiers, drawn up in martial array, awaited the arrival of the smugglers in front of the Red Lion. At last these daring adventurers were observed to approach, not, however, at full speed, but at a walking pace. Apparently not taking the slightest notice of the soldiers, they coolly guided their horses into the western entrance of the hotel yard. Excisemen and soldiers were now confident of their game, and at once closed upon them. The wary smugglers were not thus, however, to be captured. Instead of being caught in a trap, they were perpetrating a practical joke. They entered the hotel yard on the western side to go out at the eastern, and thence they emerged and galloped off, no doubt laughing in their sleeves, if not aloud, much to the chagrin and discomfiture of their would-be captors.

It must be five and forty years ago that a butcher's shop on the same side of the street was transformed by its proprietor into the "Jolly Brewers" beerhouse, and almost the same since the Sun Brewery and its retail establishment were founded.

The old Market House, once standing in the roadway near the Red Lion, with its grated cells for prisoners, its stocks, its store-room for corn, and its fire-bell, had disappeared before I can remember. Before this, too, the fine old Dutch House, a little lower down, had been modernised and spoilt. The Three Tuns Inn, which has of late years put on an improved appearance, was, half a century ago, as now, the site of the Corn Market. Then, however, a large portion of its ground floor was devoted to the "pitching" of grain. Outside of the old inn there was once a seat, or settle, of considerable length, for the accommodation of customers and the public. Varied in type and calling were the well-known characters who, in years gone by, visited the market. Among the more noted of these was a rat-catcher, who announced his vocation by a belt with the motto, "Death to the rats," but who, it is stated, showed his tender regard for the vermin, or rather for himself, by saying to the boys who aided him, "Don't kill *all* of them, but *some* of them, or my trade will be gone." Another noted character was a gaunt-looking man, who, with combs, brushes, and scissors peeping from his pockets, performed in the open air, upon some of the market attendants, seated on a three-legged stool, the operation of hair-cutting. Then there was poor blind Tom, from Epsom, who used to visit Dorking on market and other days, and who showed such wonderful ability in selecting colours for his basket work, in his knowledge of the road between the two towns, and in his quick recognition of familiar voices. The little shop, approached by three or four brick steps, lately displaced by the new bank of the Hampshire Banking Company, was, fifty years ago, that of a fishmonger. Here, at the top of the steps, the corpulent proprietor of this establishment used to sit on a summer's evening, chatting with the passers by, enjoying, meanwhile, sundry and divers whiffs from his favourite "churchwarden." The Black Horse, like its neighbour a little higher up, has a renovated aspect, since the time when its ground floor was crammed with "pitched" corn, and when the buyer and seller were intently occupied in testing the quality and settling the price. The old candle factory, then in operation close by here, has now for some years ceased to exist. The White Horse Inn (now hotel) although more attractive and more extensive than it was, presents, in its general outline, a similar appearance to the hostelry of bygone times. The then dilapidated little building at its side has been absorbed into the hotel, and the old elder tree in front has long since disappeared. Still earlier was the disappearance of a flourishing barberry, which, we are told, once grew by the adjoining old Dutch House. The respected landlord of the White Horse, half a century ago, and for many years after, was Mr William Penn, who, it is stated, claimed a lineal descent from his namesake, the great Quaker and founder of Pennsylvania. The greatest change in Mill Lane, now called Mill Street, is at the lower part of it. Here the site of the present brewery was, and had been, from time immemorial, a tanner's yard, the workmen in which, two centuries ago, tradition says, escaped the plague, which was then so frightfully and so generally prevalent among the inhabitants. The predecessor of the residence east of the

Mill Street entrance, was, we are told, quite an ancient-looking one, with a row of trees in front of it. Fifty years ago, two low-built tenements, with doors divided into two, and with old-fashioned shop windows, supported by wooden posts, stood on a part of the site of the high houses hard by. One of these little establishments was that of a watchmaker, and the other of a turner and carpenter. Eastward of these habitations was an old blacksmith's shop, with a pent-house in front, where the horses were shod. The Ram Inn, an old hostelry, which has existed for many a day, has, of late years, had a renovated exterior. It is said of the signboard of the old inn that it was formerly suspended across the road, from a tree which stood in front of the house, and from another on the opposite side. The solicitor's office, facing the Ram Inn, was then, as now, that of the Clerk to the Magistrates, which post, half a century ago, was held, as it had then been, we believe, for some time previously, by the late Mr. Thomas Hart, on whose decease, now about forty years ago, the same important and responsible office devolved upon his son, Mr. John Hart, the present holder of it. The "Surrey Yeoman," a name given to the Inn, probably out of compliment to the nobleman who once lived in the adjacent mansion, is but little altered in fifty years. This, too, is evidently a very old inn. One is curious to know whether this, or the "Ram," might not have been anciently the "Little Chequers," for an old deed, if we mistake not, of the seventeenth century, refers to the right of some old cottages once standing on the site of the White Hart, in Dene Street, to the use of a well, belonging to an Inn, then called the "Little Chequers." Near to the "Surrey Yeoman," and on the same side of the road, might be seen, in bygone years, a weaver, sitting by his shop window, busily plying his shuttle, exciting the curiosity of the juveniles, and attracting the attention of other passers-by. More than forty years have passed since lectures were delivered under the auspices of the Dorking Mechanics' Institution at the old Infant Schoolroom, and since a spirited meeting was thrilled there by the eloquent denunciation of the West India Apprenticeship Act by that friend of the Slave and Slavery Abolition, John Scoble. About the same time, too, the inhabitants of the town were not a little excited by an outbreak of Asiatic cholera in the neighbouring cottages. Somewhere near the same period, the coach factory, a little to the eastward, superseded a chimney-sweeper's sooty establishment, which establishment it is said was hastily vacated by its proprietor, who, pursued by an officer of justice, escaped apprehension by wading the adjacent stream, and was never seen in Dorking again. We have already noticed Shrub Hill; we pass on, therefore, to the residence, now known as the Grammar School, where, fifty years and more ago, dwelt Mr. Joseph Moore, then an active and prominent parochial politician, and whose residence here, without doubt, gave to the adjacent thoroughfare the name of "Moore's Lane." In the same house, also, at a more recent period, lived, after her return from abroad, the late genial and popular Lady Elizabeth Wathen. Ram Alley, or, as it is now called, Dene Street, though improved in some parts of it, does not appear to call for special notice. It may be interesting to say, however, that an old inhabitant has told me that a wooden rail once extended from the entrance of the alley to some distance up, for the protection of footpath passengers. Cotmandene, or as it was formerly called, the Heath, has more habitations around it than it had fifty years ago, for the villas on its western side, and some of the cottages on the eastern were not then erected. The old almshouses of that period have since given place to a larger number of new ones, erected on and near their site. The old summer house close by the almshouses was once used as an ammunition depôt of the Surrey Yeomanry Cavalry. A road then ran between the Deepdene Gardens towards Park Farm. The proposal made some forty years ago to close this highway and give in lieu of it the present one through Chart Park, excited a spirited and strenuous opposition. Various squibs and jokes anent the question were circulated, and no little ill-feeling was created, but ultimately the proposal was legally ratified, and thus one of the pleasantest walks near the town was thenceforward lost. The cluster of noble old limes, then called "The moon trees," and the elms on the other side of the cricketing ground, designated "The half moon trees," yet exist. It was beneath these old trees that the booths were erected, from which excited spectators viewed the matches, and cheered the cricketers in bygone years. About these contests, however, and the great Reform dinner which took place at the same spot, I intend to say more by-and-by. What a variety of spectacles the old Dene has witnessed! Here in the quietude of the morning, and in inhaling "the finest air in England," the invalid has sought the blessing of health. And here, in contrast to this, have been the noisy gambols of boisterous mirth. Here, too, have been sights of marvellous curiosities, of clever feats of horsemanship, of the laughable, but not always innocent tricks, of itinerant Merry-andrews. One of the most extraordinary and unprincipled acts of the last-named to draw an audience, was perhaps the following:—The clown of a mountebank company, about to perform on the Dene, many a year ago, promised to give to any owner of a perfectly black dog a pound of tea. This, from the high price of the article at that period, was an offer by no means to be despised, and, tempted by it, old ladies and others possessing animals of this colour, wended their way to the exhibition, not only from the immediate neighbourhood, but from the villages around. Assured that the pet dog was an entirely jet one, and, confident of the prize, what pleasurable anticipations there were that morning of neighbourly greetings and cozy chattings over the wished-for tea! Alas! however, how human hopes are sometimes disappointed! The prize appeared in sight, but was not yet in hand. Each dog, on arriving at the spot, had to undergo a scrutinizing examination within the mountebank enclosure, the owners meanwhile waiting outside till the ordeal was over. To some this must have been ominous, and to all a trial of patience. At length the announcement was made that on every dog a white spot had been discovered, and on every one a white spot certainly appeared. The competitors were puzzled and bewildered. They, too, had examined the animals, in some cases again and again, but had never seen the spot before. Ultimately, however, the mystery was solved, the spot was not there naturally; the rascally clown had painted it. To some the trick might have been ludicrous, but it was too bad, it was dishonest.

A GENERAL REVIEW OF THE TOWN.

SOUTH STREET.—THE PARISH CONSTABLE AND THE COMMERCIAL TRAVELLER.—THE ORIGIN OF CHOPSTICK PLACE.—A FUNNY ACCIDENT TO THE WORKHOUSE GOVERNOR.

Let us now visit South Street. Here, at its eastern entrance, stands the White Lion, with a somewhat improved exterior, since when, on Saturday nights, in years gone by, its doorway was besieged by workmen employed at the Chalk Pits, and in building operations, by the late Mr. Samuel Bothwell, and who were waiting here to attend that welcome spot—the pay table.

That formerly and still well-ordered hostelry, the Bull's Head, if we except the recent improvement in its doorway, has been but little altered in fifty years. It is now, however, no longer the scene of animation that it was in the old coaching days, when the horses were changed, and seaside visitors, on their way down or up from Brighton, Worthing, Bognor, and Littlehampton, welcomed a break in their journey, and dined at the inn. This, too, was a favourite resort for many a comfort-loving "commercial," to one of whom here a singular adventure once occurred. The gentleman in question, taking time by the forelock, had travelled from Horsham to Dorking before breakfast. He was about to sit down to his morning meal, when the parish constable from the first-named town confronted him, and a conversation, somewhat as follows, then took place: "You slept at Horsham last night," quoth the constable, "and at such an inn." "I did; and what of that?" was the reply. "You are charged with stealing the sheets of the bed you slept in," retorted the officer. "Sit down to breakfast with me," said the good-natured traveller, "and I will tell you all about it." "I found," said he, "when I was about to get into bed that the sheets were so damp as to be utterly unfit to sleep between. I therefore placed them on the Turk's head besom and thrust them up the chimney, and there the landlord will find them; and you tell him from me never again to risk people's health and lives by putting damp sheets into their beds." It is almost unnecessary to add that after this ample explanation our friend the "commercial" escaped being arrested. The site of the Rotunda was, fifty years ago, a walled enclosure, within which grew some thriving horse chestnut trees. Exactly in front of the western end of this enclosure stood that once dreaded instrument of punishment for rogues and vagabonds, the stocks. A story is told of two offenders who were punished here at the same time, one of whom exclaimed to the other, "They had no right to put us here." His companion, however, probably conscious of his deserts, and more submissive to his fate, retorted, "But they have done it." The old white house, with the palisades in front, and facing eastwards, was forty years ago, and for some time after, the residence of Mr. John Beckett, whose oil paintings of the old

Parish Church, and other ancient but now demolished erections, and of some of the prettiest views in the neighbourhood, have been justly admired, and are now greatly prized. The designation, Butter Hill, now restricted to the elevation on the left hand, was, many years ago, applied to the eastern portion of South Street in general. The building on the top of the hill, utilised at the present time as a storehouse for corn, was, many years ago, used as a spirit distillery. Butter Hill and its immediate neighbourhood was, fifty years ago, and, with one exception about that time, had been—indeed from time immemorial—the annual scene of the Pleasure Fair. The years of my earliest remembrance of the fair, however, were palmy ones, compared with those immediately preceding its removal to the more capacious and convenient region of Cotmandene. It must be almost, or quite, forty years, since the Spotted Dog first appeared, somewhat higher up the street. For many a year before this, the old brewery, once in operation a little to the southward, had sent forth its XXX, while the crystal spring in the cave opposite was there then, and had been, in all probability, long before. Half a century ago the old Pound, a walled enclosure, with a wooden barred gate, stood on the site of the Police Station. An odd discovery was made here in years gone by, for a cart laden with osiers, which the evening before had stood outside the Pound, was found the next morning with its load upon it, within the enclosure. By what means this had been accomplished was at first a puzzle, for the Pound gateway was utterly inadequate to admit the vehicle. It transpired afterwards that the act was a prank of the practical jokers who were then so busy, and who in the night had unloaded the cart, taken off its wheels, lifted over the body of the vehicle into the enclosure, and then restored the wheels and the osiers to their former position. All this must have involved considerable labour, but as it was done for a joke it was no doubt cheerfully and gleefully performed. Had the jokers been compelled to do it, their lot would, in all probability, have been thought a hard one; but working hard to perpetrate a joke, and working hard to gain a livelihood, or to do good to others, are, of course, different things. In the very old cottage opposite the Police Station has long lived a venerable widow, Mrs. Elizabeth Taylor, who, when nine years of age, now seventy six years ago, sat on the coffin of the eccentric Major Labelliere, while her younger brother danced upon it.

The upper part of Junction Road was fifty years ago a nursery ground. Stapleton House, erected, pursuant to the date on its western side, 1668, is but little changed, the chief alteration in it being an additional story to its height. Hereabouts there have been perhaps fewer changes than in any other leading thoroughfare in the town. Before leaving this locality we must just take a peep at Vincent's Walk. Passers by in the present day have, no doubt, often wondered at the odd name given to the wretched habitations at the end of the roadway. Chopstick Place received its designation now more than forty years ago on this wise: "Chopstick" was the name by which the tenant, if not the proprietor of these tenements and the adjoining wheelwright's yard was familiarly known, and one morning he found, to his amusement, his own whimsical appellation inscribed upon his premises. Suspicion as to the act at once fell upon a jocular acquaintance, who soon after discovered that the thoroughfare in which he lived, had received one night, no doubt by way of retort, the title of "Cockchaffer Lane." The obnoxious board making this announcement was, as may be readily imagined, quickly removed, but our friend "Chopstick," either from a relish of the joke that had been played upon him, or from some other cause, allowed his own queer name to remain unobliterated, and "Chopstick Place" has stuck to these miserable huts ever since.

On the brow of the hill stands Holder House, an old residence with a somewhat renovated exterior. The row of limes which fifty years ago grew in front of it, and the posts and chains which were there for some time after, have now disappeared. Eastward of this residence, and close by it, is the "Hole-in-the-Wall," an old cottage, where lived and died the singular Major Labelliere, and which cottage, to use the words of a venerable informant, is "not altered a bit" since the Major's remains left its doorway for their last resting place on Box Hill. A little further to the southward of Holder House, on the right hand side of the road, opposite the stone wall, on which grew then, as now, the pellitory, stood the old Workhouse. This erection was a brick one of considerable length, with leaden casement windows, and of the plainest style of architecture. It stood some yards distant from the road and was approached by an entrance down some steps, on the right hand of which were some very ancient habitations, built, if I mistake not, of wood and what used to be called "wattle and dab." The site of these dwellings is now occupied by the butcher's shop. On the left hand side of the entrance was the Cage, a name at the present day more suggestive of a receptacle for the safe keeping of winged songsters, than a place for gaol birds. The Cage was a low strong brick-built and slated-roofed building, divided into two compartments, each, of course, having its heavily barred door, and enclosed by a stronger outer one. The old Workhouse itself was pulled down soon after the erection of the Union House, now about forty years ago, but an erection close by it, and which was used for the same purposes was transformed into tenements, still stands. The post of "Governor" of the Workhouse, for such the manager was called, was held, half a century ago, by Mr. Jesse Beecham. Mr Beecham's predecessor, I have heard, was Mr. Boyce, whom some untoward incident had deprived of a leg, and whom art had supplied with a wooden one. In the Workhouse, while Mr. Boyce was Governor, was a youth who had suffered a similar deprivation, and whom art had furnished in like manner with a substitute. This youth, who years afterwards held the post of town crier, was of a facetious disposition, and imitated the Governor in his movements so exactly, as to excite the merriment of all in the House. The Governor, good man, seems to have been of a speculative turn, for he tried his fortune in one of the Lotteries of the period, and, what he no doubt considered better, was successful. His share, it is true, was only the fraction of a prize. Great was his joy, however, at hearing the news, and sad was the result, for, filled to overflowing with delight, he danced and capered about so vigorously that he broke his wooden leg! Possibly the incident may have been remembered by his wooden-legged junior, when in years after, the latter met more than once with a similar disaster, at one time through the slipping of his wooden support one day, or rather one night, into one of the blind-stick holes in the High Street, and when he needed for himself, or rather for his wooden leg, the skill in restoring that he professed to exercise in his "umbrella and parasol hospital." After the demolition of the Workhouse, the Cage was still used for the detention of accused persons, and continued to be so till the erection of the Police Station. The brewery in operation, fifty years ago, a little further to the southward, gave place, some time since, to the dwelling houses now standing on its site. "The

Cricketers" was originated at a later period by one of the junior members of the Old Dorking Eleven. The old-fashioned comfortable-looking brick residence, with the limes, grass plat, and palisades in front, is almost unchanged from the time it was so many years occupied by the late Mr. James Bravery, who once, during his long career as a miller, and while on his way from Horsham market, was attacked by highwaymen, and whose end, it was stated, was accelerated, if not absolutely caused by the excitement and anxiety incident to an incendiary fire at his mill at Westcott. The site of the next residence, on the same side of the road, was long used as a market garden, while that of the adjoining greenhouse was, fifty years ago, a bricklayer's yard. At the eastern end of the dwelling house, close by, was, for many years, a flourishing pear tree. There is, perhaps, no residence in the town which has been less changed by the lapse of time than the old Vicarage, occupied during his long vicariate by the Rev. George Feachem. The dwelling itself, the iron fence in front, the ivied wall, and all the other surroundings, are, in fact, all but the same as when, half a century ago, the good Vicar, clad in knee-breeches and silk stockings, and with the upper garments and head gear worn by clergymen of the olden time, emerged from the gateway to "do duty" at the church, or to visit, it might be, some of the afflicted ones of his flock. I well remember him thus habited, when, four-and-forty years ago, he left his residence very early in the morning, to plead and remonstrate with an indebted parishioner just about to start for America. The intending emigrant had not paid his vicarial tithes, and, notwithstanding the good Vicar's warning, that the blessing of God could never be expected under such circumstances, the tithe-owing parishioner departed from Dorking without satisfying the demand made upon him. Let us now take a glance along the road towards Vincent's Lane. The old bakehouse of fifty years ago, on the left hand, has disappeared, and the mansion on the same side of the road, has, during that period, been greatly enlarged and improved. The site of the brick-built houses a little beyond was the old route of the turnpike, before its diversion to the present one by the Queen's Head Inn. This alteration, it appears, was carried out at the expense of the then Duke of Norfolk, who offered, on the demolition of the old Market House, either to erect a new one, or to effect this improvement, and the inhabitants of the time gave a preference to the latter. Opposite these villas was an old cottage residence, which had stood there for many a generation. So, too, had two or three little old tenements, which, in years gone by, occupied the site of the villa at the corner. Hereabouts, in fact, all is change, and this has swept away the two snug old cottages which, with the well in front, and the box hedge at the side, had so long stood at the top of the lane.

Our review of the town is now completed.

THE ANCIENT DIVISIONS AND MANAGEMENT OF THE TOWN AND PARISH.

THE OLD OFFICERS.—THE HIGH CONSTABLE.—THE PARISH CONSTABLE.—THE HEADBOROUGHS.—THE PATROL.—THE ALE-TASTER.—THE "BEGGAR POKERS."—THE BEADLE AND CRIER.

The parish of Dorking was anciently divided into boroughs. It is stated that at one time there were six, and at another two. Fifty years ago there were four—Chipping, East or Betchworth, Westcott, and Holmwood. Chipping Borough included South Street, West Street, and Back Lane; East, or Betchworth Borough, comprehended High Street, London Road, and the eastern part of the parish generally. Westcott Borough included the village bearing that name and the other western portions of the parish. Holmwood Borough in like manner comprehended the Holmwood and its northern, eastern, and western surroundings. In the last-named borough was comprised also, by one of those strange freaks sometimes incident to boundary lines, a fraction of the parish near the Chalk Pits. By the legislative changes of late years these divisions of the parish are now for practical purposes rendered well-nigh obsolete. Fifty years ago, however, it was far otherwise, for then the boroughs were the boundaries within which some of the parish officials exercised special functions. Thus, to each borough was assigned a headborough for the performance of constabulary duties, a waywarden to look after the highways, and an overseer to take the oversight of the poor. Upon the two last-named officers devolved the duty of collecting the highway rate and the poor rate respectively, and this without receiving any pecuniary remuneration. With such innocent confidence were these matters then managed that no separate statement of the rate was rendered, nor any receipt given, it being thought quite sufficient that the ratepayer should see the sum charged in the rate-book, and that the amount he had tendered had been entered in the "sums received" column. Sometimes, when it was inconvenient for the officer himself to undertake personally the duty of collection, a substitute, perhaps too juvenile, would be deputed for the purpose. I remember that when a youth this task was more than once assigned to me, and that on one occasion I was saluted with the question, "Why doesn't your father collect the rate himself, and not send such a boy as you?" My reception in other cases was more courteous, and was sometimes spiced with a little good-humoured pleasantry. For instance, when one day announcing to an elderly kind-hearted lady that I had called for the highway rate, she at once paid it, with the jocular remark, "Tell your father I didn't know that he was a highwayman!" A curious legal requirement at that time existed. I refer to the liability of those who kept horses and carts and other vehicles to a "six days' statute duty upon the highways." In lieu of this duty a composition was determined by the Justices in Special Sessions. From an old highway rate-book now before me, it is shown that one of the most recent of these composition tariffs for this parish was fixed by the Justices at their Sessions held October 6th, 1834. Whether there was any truth in the statement sometimes made that the waywardens exercised a special care over the highways near their own homesteads or those of their friends I will not say. Were it so, the appointment of a Highway Board under a subsequent Act of Parliament prevented the likelihood of such favouritism in future, and, in fact, provided for a better management of the highways. The overseers, fifty years ago, had other heavy duties besides the collecting of the poor rate. About these, however, and about the functions of the other parish officers, I must speak more fully in a future paper. As already intimated, these ancient parish landmarks—the boroughs—are now of little practical use. They belonged to a time when each citizen was expected and called upon to give his time and services, often undoubtedly at too great a sacrifice, for the common weal. Modern legislation, embodying the real or supposed requirements of modern society, is fast changing all this. What was formerly done patriotically and without remuneration is now, in fact, to a great extent performed by the paid functionary.

Fifty years ago the holding in the autumn of the Court Leet at the Red Lion Hotel was an important event. At the same time and place the Court Baron, another Court of the Manor of Dorking, was also held. Both these Courts have of late years ceased to be holden. At the Court Leet "a presentment was made of nuisances, encroachments, and offences against the Crown," which matters were then and there severally dealt with. At this Court, also, the appointment of parish constables and headboroughs for the year was made. I well remember with what anxiety in the troublous times of five-and-forty years ago the announcement as to the assignment of these offices was expected; in fact, the onerous duty then devolving on constable and headborough, and the perils and dangers to which they were frequently exposed, rendered these offices the reverse of being coveted ones. The headboroughs, as already stated, were the peace officers of the several boroughs of the parish. Over the headboroughs was the petty constable, whose district of legal authority was the parish. Superior to, and over all these, was the high constable, whose jurisdiction extended to the entire Hundred—the Hundred of Wotton. The petty or parish constable, and the headboroughs, were alike charged with the duty of arresting offenders, and of taking them, when summarily convicted, to the treadmill at Brixton, or, when committed for trial, to some other county prison. In addition to these duties, it devolved on the petty constable to provide for the billeting of soldiers and the impressment of waggons and horses for the transit of arms, ammunition, and baggage. These duties, from the frequent military movements of from forty to fifty years ago, were then by no means light. The office of high constable was, I believe, formerly an annual one, but in later years it became practically a permanent one, and was most efficiently filled, from the year 1833 till the time of his decease—a period of forty years—by the late Mr. James White. The symbol of the high constable's office was a mace, and of the petty constable's a small staff, a few inches long, with the Royal Arms emblazoned upon it. The latter officer and the headboroughs were armed for self-defence with a large staff, and sometimes with pistols. The high constable had once a year to appear at the Assizes or Quarter Sessions to answer to the call of his name. In addition to his being officially responsible for the peace of the Hundred, it was his function also to convene and preside at public meetings of the inhabitants, the preliminary procedure in such cases being a requisition to him for that purpose. The last public occasion on which the late high constable exercised the duties of his office was on the celebration of the marriage of the Prince of Wales. On Mr. White's decease, the office of high constable lapsed, and is now virtually, if not legally, abolished. It is much to be regretted that, with the abrogation of the office, the town no longer possesses a recognised head through whom legitimately to express its opinion on any Imperial or local question. Dorking, in fact, notwithstanding its growing importance, is in this respect no better off than a third-class village.

It seems almost incredible that little more than fifty years ago the tradesmen of Dorking, in the absence of a legislative provision for the purpose, took their turns in watching the town at night. Yet an old inhabitant states that such was the fact, and that he well remembers his father going out at night to take his accustomed "beat." This arrangement not only involved considerable personal sacrifice and inconvenience, but was evidently found to be in its working an inexpedient one. A meeting of the inhabitants was therefore held on the 7th of November, 1825, "for the purpose of establishing a nightly patrol, for the protection of the town and neighbourhood." I glean from an old minute-book, which has been kindly lent to me, that at this meeting a committee was appointed to solicit subscriptions to a patrol fund, and to nominate and superintend the patrol. Among other interesting records in the old document referred to, it is stated that the watchmen were instructed to cry the hour, and my earliest reminiscences are associated with this memorable usage. Thus with the measured tramp of the patrol there would be the cry, as the case might require, "Past eleven!" or "Past one!" and sometimes the added announcement, "and a cloudy night" or "a starlight morning." This crying of the hour, though reassuring to the inhabitants as to the fidelity and presence of the watchman, had, of course, the disadvantage of warning the burglar of the officer's approach, and of intimating to the depredator when he might with greater safety resume his operations. Somewhat in contrast to the heralding of their approach by the crying of the hour the patrols were each presented with a pair of shoes, "with soles stitched instead of nailed, for use when on duty." the object of this presentation apparently being the obtainment of greater quietness during the watchman's movements. Each patrol was furnished with a rattle, and was paid half-a-crown for each night's services. The hours of duty varied at different periods. Thus one patrol was appointed to be on duty from 10 p.m. to 5 a.m., and the other two alternately from 8 till 4 and 11 to 6 o'clock. One or two years one of the patrols was kept on duty through the summer, while on Saturday nights and at Fair time the watchmen were on special duty. The first two patrols appointed were George Stonestreet and James Bowshell, and to these was added, a short time afterwards, Charles Langton. The first-named proved so efficient at his post, that three years after his first appointment he was made a Bow Street Runner—an officer whose very name, half a century ago, struck terror into the hearts of rogues and thieves in general. Although Patrol Stonestreet was thus promoted, he was not unmindful of the interests of his fellow inhabitants, for he offered still to render aid to his old comrades in case of emergency, and this offer, it need hardly be said, was gladly accepted. The year following the institution of the patrol, an attempted robbery of one of the banks occurred, but an investigation into the circumstances perfectly exonerated the officers from negligence of duty. After this, however, it was thought wise that one of the patrol should keep within the precincts of the town. The object designed in the appointment of the patrol seems to have been satisfactorily attained, for the old record alluded to states, in the spring of 1828, that in the previous winter there had been "an absence of all depredation." The Patrol Committee if not charged at first with the care of the street lamps, afterwards had this duty confided to them, and it is not a little interesting to learn that, so comparatively late as 1830, they should have requested tenders for "pure seal oil." Soon after this, however, a new order of things was introduced, and gas superseded oil, and the police the old patrol. The two watchmen, for several years before the abolition of the office, were Patrol Thomas Peters and Patrol Richard Rose, the former of whom died two or three years ago, and the last-named of whom still survives.

Another old and now obsolete officer in Dorking was the ale-taster. This functionary, like the constable and headboroughs, was appointed by the Court Leet. He was "sworn to look to the assize (or regulation of the price), and the goodness of bread, and of ale, or beer, within the precincts of the lordship." The office was held about fifty years ago by the late Mr. Phillip Cooke, but, as we have said, is now obsolete.

There is yet another old officer of half a century ago whose functions are now superseded—the beggar-poker, or as he was vulgarly called, "the beggar-pooker." And who on earth, a recent resident may ask, was the beggar-poker? He was a very respectable person in his way, a kind of sub-beadle, without uniform, generally an elderly man, who had seen better days, who, armed with a painted pole about five feet long, warned the beggars to move on, and who, if it were necessary, escorted them, like a guard of honour, to the outside of the town. Whether their staff of office was ever used in the way of poking the more sturdy of the mendicants, I cannot say, but this I do know, that I have often seen these officers parade the streets, and that they were known by everybody in the place as the "beggar-pokers," or the "beggar-pookers."

The offices of town crier and beadle, fifty years ago, were held by the same person. The town crier of that period was an important-looking personage, for unlike the crier of the present day, he was dressed in becoming official costume—a gold-braided beadle's hat, and a caped gold-braided coat, while in his hand was his wand of office. Old John Chamberlain, whose tall and portly form well became the office, filled the post for many years. To him succeeded, from forty to five-and-forty years ago, Thomas Thompson, who still donned the braided coat, but exchanged the beadle's hat for one of a chimney-pot shape, and having round it a gold band. I well remember when Crier Thompson, with bell and hat in hand, announced his appointment to the office, which office he was to hold "during good behaviour." It is to be feared, however, that the poor crier's love of something stronger than water, made it doubtful afterwards whether this "good behaviour" was, at all times, maintained. One of Crier Thompson's most memorable appearances was on the Queen's Coronation Day, and although happening somewhat later than the prescribed range of my "recollections," I am tempted to narrate it. There had been during the day an unwonted absence of loyal demonstration on the part of the inhabitants.

This, however, it is only right to state, was afterwards explained to have arisen from a determination on the part of some of the leading residents of the place to celebrate the event by gifts to charitable objects, rather than by an expenditure for decorations during the day, and an illumination in the evening. The omission of a loyal demonstration was, however, a fact, and, disappointed and annoyed by it, some of the inhabitants determined, by a public announcement, to express their disapprobation. Crier Thompson was the official through whom they could legitimately express their dissatisfaction, and he was the very man to carry out their wishes. With crape around his hat and staff, and himself not in the condition of a total abstainer, he went round the town in the afternoon, crying as he went, in a doleful tone, "Lost! lost! lost! The loyalty of Dorking; whosoever has the same, and will display it to-day, shall receive the reward of a good Sovereign." However applicable, or inapplicable, the first part of the crier's announcement may have been, all loyal subjects will cordially agree that the prognostic contained in the closing sentence has been happily and thoroughly fulfilled.

THE ANCIENT MANAGEMENT OF THE TOWN AND PARISH.

The Select and Parish Vestries.—The Overseers and their Duties.—The Parish Charities.

Fifty years ago the parish affairs generally were managed by a Select Vestry. This body, if I remember rightly, was not a popular one, and it was ultimately abolished. When the management of affairs reverted to the parishioners in general, now five and forty years or more ago, the vestry meetings were usually of a stormy nature; for at this period the contention between the town and the farmers, in all matters in which their interests were not identical, was hot and severe. The latter had two or three of their number who advocated their cause with considerable ability and energy, while the town was by no means weakly represented. These conflicts gave rise to an ill-feeling which not unfrequently displayed itself. "Ye townspeople are always *aginst* the farmers, ever doth," was the characteristic utterance of a sturdy, but not accomplished agriculturist of the period. This sentiment, there is reason to believe, was then shared by the tillers of the soil in general. Happily, however, these asperities between the agricultural and the town ratepayers have long ceased.

The duties of the Overseers of fifty years ago were, as already intimated, indeed arduous compared with those of the Overseers of to-day. These officers, like those of the present time, were aided by a paid functionary known then as the Fifth Overseer. At that period the sole supervision of the Workhouse devolved on the Overseers, who showed their consideration for its aged inmates, by granting to them weekly "gratuities" of tobacco, snuff, &c. The inmates generally, in fact, fared considerably better than those of the Union Houses of the present day, or indeed than many an industrious and hard working family outside the precincts of these establishments. Were proof of this necessary it is to be found in the following incident. A labouring man who had just been to the Overseers for parish relief, met, on his return home, an acquaintance who was then in the Workhouse. The latter accosted the former, familiarly inquired if he wasn't coming into the "house," for, said the inmate, "We have just had in a bullock, and we shall live well for the next month." The Overseers of the period referred to, adopted the custom which then prevailed, of dispensing the parish funds on Sunday afternoons at the close of Divine Service. Numbers of the poor might then be seen entering the vestry-room of the parish church, or attending the Workhouse; some to apply for bread, and others, it might be, for an order for a pair of shoes, a bill-hook, a pair of hedging gloves, or other things of a similar nature. Parish relief was given, too, in the way of employment, and at the close of the week crowds of men might be observed in front of the residence of the Assistant-Overseer to receive the wages then due to them. The Workhouse or parish garden was an enclosure of considerable extent, now cultivated as an arable field to the north-west of the present Vicarage. Here the aged male inmates of the Workhouse and others dependent upon the parish were employed, and a considerable proportion of the garden produce was disposed of by being hawked around the town. I well remember one of the aged men employed in the garden, Steer by name, who had such an extraordinary visual faculty as to be able to look at the sun for some seconds without apparent discomfort. Another place of parish employment was the Giles Green gravel pit, where scores of men, who during the winters of that period were unable to get work elsewhere, were employed. At that time, indeed, in the winter season, it was of common occurrence to witness the pitiable spectacle of large groups of unemployed mechanics and other workmen standing involuntarily idle, at and about the Post Office corner.

The wise and equitable distribution of the poor rate fund was at that period a matter of no little difficulty. A conviction of the right to parish relief, not only in times of urgency, but at others also, was pertinaciously held by the poorer class in general. This often rendered its members clamorous and unreasoning, and led to an undue increase of the ratepayers' burdens. So great indeed was the terrorism then exercised by the pauperised class that the parish officers, after a refusal of the demands made upon them, were sometimes afraid of personal violence on their way home. It is not to be wondered at that under circumstances like these, with what appears now an almost incredible number receiving parochial relief, and with a lavish expenditure in the Workhouse like that referred to, the poor rate should have been enormously high; so high indeed that Mr. Timbs, in his *Promenade Round Dorking*, states that in 1817 it was no less than eight shillings in the £. This, however, it is only just to remember, was on a low basis of assessment, and at a time, too, when the rate was increased, by the large number of the "poor," including even some of the mechanics, "excused" from payment. Still the fact remains, that a very large proportion of the population lived and throve upon the industry and resources of the rest of the inhabitants. The Poor Law Amendment Act very properly put an end to such a state of affairs, although possibly there is now a danger of verging on the other extreme, in a too large administrative expenditure, and in an insufficient consideration for the really deserving yet impoverished sons and daughters of toil.

On the Overseers and Churchwardens—the latter being *ex-officio* overseers of the poor—devolved the duty also of dispensing the parish charities. This was by no means a trivial matter, especially when the varied conditions under which these gifts were bequeathed, and the numerous and conflicting claims for them were considered. Thus, while two of the more important of the charities—the Bottesford and the Chislet—were left for bread, meat, clothing, &c., for the poor generally, the Fordland Charity was bequeated specially for the apprenticing of poor children, and for marriage dowries to maid servants, living seven years in one situation. Again, the Longstock Charity was distributed among poor widows; while of the minor charities, one was bequeathed for the distribution of bread to forty poor widows on New Year's Day; and another in penny loaves to the "very needy poor," on Good Friday. The difficulties involved, and the alleged abuse in the distribution of these liberal gifts, led to the throwing of them, with one exception, into Chancery. Ultimately an order was made by the Court prescribing the future dispensation of the charities by a Board of Trustees, appointed, in the first instance, by the Court, but to be thenceforth virtually self-elective. The order also directed the appropriation of a portion of the Charities' Fund to the enlargement of the almshouses on Cotmandene, and to an increased provision for its inmates. It at the same time prescribed the continued appropriation of some of the fund to the apprenticing of boys, and to the dowries of maid servants, and the residue as "gift money" to the aged, sick, and infirm, not in the receipt of parish relief. The partial diversion of the charities from the objects designed by the donors, though ostensibly justified by expediency, involves a principle of considerable importance. Whatever may be said in favour of the State's restraining the "dead man's hand," such restraint, in the case of our own parish, had, at least, one disadvantage, for it is said that it deterred the late Mr. Denison from adding, as he had intended, to these testamentary bequests. When, however, the diversion of the charities already existing had been accomplished, he declined to carry out his purpose, remarking, at the time, that after so undesigned an appropriation of these bequests, it was useless to leave anything for such an object, as no one could tell to what purpose it might be ultimately applied. I will just add that, fifty years ago, there was a singular application of the parish funds, for at that period a grant was made from one of the rates for the heads of sparrows and other winged depredators of the garden, orchard, and corn field.

THE OLD PLACES OF WORSHIP.

Old St. Martin's Church.

Half a century ago the places of worship in Dorking were indeed few, compared with those that exist now. Old, or as it may be called, ancient St. Martin's Church, was then the sole Episcopalian church, in and for the entire parish. The only other places of worship in the parish were the Independent and Friends' (or Quakers') Meeting Houses in West Street, and the small Calvinistic one near the Holmwood Windmill. The old church of St. Martin's was then attended by parishioners residing at the Holmwood and at Coldharbour and Westcott. Some of the residents in the western portion of the latter, however, went to the neighbouring Church of Wotton. As already stated the late Mr. John Beckett executed an oil painting of Old St. Martin's, which is generally regarded as a faithful picture. The old inhabitants well remember the ancient edifice with its stone-covered roof, its old-fashioned tower, its capacious southern porch, and its fine old traceried western window. The old edifice, without and within, presented an appearance of great antiquity. It looked, in fact, quite as ancient as the date assigned for its erection, in Brayley's " History of Surrey "—the period of Richard the Second. The entrance to the church was by the descent of steps. There were two or three at the doorway of the southern porch —the principal entrance—and one or two more after the porch was passed, at the entrance to the aisle. Within the church stone arches, with massive piers, divided the nave from the aisles. The upper part of some of the arches forming, in fact, a part of the gallery, was appropriated as pews by the nobility and gentry. The same portion of some of the remaining arches, towards the western portion of the building, was occupied by the congregation in general. In one of the galleries—the western—was stationed the choir, partly instrumental and partly vocal, who, when engaged at their duties, were screened from the public gaze by green baize curtains. Opposite the western gallery was the comparatively small door way, with glazed doors, which led to the chancel. The pulpit, which is said to have been of the seventeenth century, was of oak, and at its foot was the reading desk, and lower down still the clerk's desk. The font was a plain stone one, situated beneath the gallery, and near the western entrance. The edifice was lighted chiefly by the fine old western window which, with the other windows, was glazed with small diamond panes of transparent glass. Two large massive brass candelabra were suspended in the middle of the nave for artificial light when needed. On the wall separating the nave from the chancel, were full-length paintings of Moses and Aaron; the last-named with a censer, and arrayed as a Jewish High Priest, the former with a rod in his hand, and attired as one of the old prophets. Around the walls of the nave were hung the memorial hatchments of the rich, and a list of the parish charities bequeathed to the poor. Here, too, were inscribed in gilt letters, on boards painted black, the Ten Commandments, the Belief, and the Lord's Prayer. The piers of the arches, several feet in thickness, entirely obstructed the view of the reader, or preacher, from a not inconsiderable portion of the congregation. The old high oak pews, brown with age, and in some instances lined with baize, once green or crimson, proved equally obstructive to those of small stature at a distance from the desk. Indeed, it was only when the congregation stood up that the adults thus circumstanced could see the reader, while the poor children who were present had to stand upon the seats, or were doomed to sleep or otherwise pass away the time as best they could. The services, fifty years ago, were of the plain character, incident to the period. The minister, at the conclusion of the liturgical part of the service, retired to exchange the surplice for a black gown, in which he preached. The services on Sunday were restricted to the morning and afternoon. A special collection was made among the parishioners for the "afternoon lecture." On Wednesday and Friday mornings there were prayers only. The Communion Service was celebrated at the close of the morning one, on the first Sunday of every month, and on the great festivals of the Church. Twice during the year the church was decorated—on Easter Sunday with yew, and on Christmas Day, of course, with holly. The decorations were generally without artistic design, and were composed chiefly of sprigs of the evergreen placed on the pulpit, the reading and clerk's desks, and the pews in general. The two candelabra, however, received a larger share of attention. The Psalms for the day were invariably read, and the Te Deum usually so. Sometimes, however, the latter, or the Gloria, or an Anthem, would be sung, but the musical part of the service was generally restricted to the singing of two of the metrical Psalms of Tate and Brady. The Responses and the other parts of the Liturgy devolving upon the congregation were led by the clerk, Mr. John Paul Cleere, in the tone, and with the manner then characterising parish clerks in general. The clerk, too, announced the Psalms, and when the choir were absent in the afternoon, would, aided only by his daughter, who stood in the desk with him, then sing them, one of these sacred compositions beginning thus,

> " I will regard and think upon
> The goodness of the Lord,"

being with them a special favourite. The instruments used by the choir consisted of flute, clarionet, violoncello, double bass, and bassoon. It was the custom of the choir on the decease of one of their number to do honour to his memory at the funeral by the singing of an anthem. On one of these occasions, it appears, they were authoritatively ordered to desist, but refused to comply with the summons. At another time, when offended by something, their independence was manifested by their failing to appear in their places at church. A reconciliation was, however, brought about by some of the congregation, and was ratified by a supper given to the choir at one of the Inns. On another occasion, a member of the choir was unable from some cause to make his instrument sound the required note. "Let me get a fire-brand," said a sitter by, " and then it will go off." This remark was too much for the vexed musician, who, it is said, thereupon laid down his instrument, and never took his place in the choir again. It was customary for the instrumentalists before taking their part in the service to test the condition of their instruments. The jingling thus produced, however, was by no means so discordant with the solemnity of worship as the loud sounding of the beadle's cane on the back of some unruly culprit, and the shout which was thereupon uttered in the direction of the school children. Then, too, the law required the giving out of parish notices, and the announcement of other secular matters in the church during Divine service. Nor about that time was it thought to be an act of impropriety for the crier, immediately after the service was over, to mount a tomb near the church door, ring lustily his bell, shout " O, yes! O, yes! O, yes! This is to give notice," and announce the prospective holding of the Courts Leet and Baron. Strange though such things may appear to the present generation, yet at the time they were enacted they were regarded as matters of course. Nor were they peculiar to Old St. Martin's alone, for its services, though so far from perfect, would have favourably compared with the churches of the neighbouring parishes. Time, in its onward course, brought, however, its changes, and the old choir designated somewhat harshly, "an unruly gang of volunteers," was superseded by a new and powerful organ, played afterwards for many years by Mr. J. E. R. Russell. The old clerk, too, who has received a *sweeping* condemnation scarcely merited, gave place to a new and exemplary one in Mr. Henry Lanham, while the old church itself, after seeing the lapse of centuries, and the passing away of many generations, was at last doomed to demolition. Before taking a farewell of the old edifice, however, I must not omit to notice the marvellous feats of the assistant sexton—poor lame-handed John Cleere, the clerk's son. Though deprived utterly of the use of one hand, the young man referred to would, with wondrous dexterity and correctness, chime the bells for church. This he ingeniously managed to do by pulling one bell-rope with his able hand, another with one of his feet, and the third with the other foot, or, it is said, with his teeth! He manifested equal ingenuity also in the digging of graves, for in excavating he made one hand do the duty performed in the case of other persons by two, and by it threw the earth over his shoulder to the grave's mouth.

A strange discovery was once made by the clerk, or his son, in the southern porch, for it was found that a number of large casks, abstracted from a cooperage then abutting on the churchyard, had been thrown over the doors into the porch. This proved to have been the work of some of the practical jokers, who, as before stated, were formerly so busy, and who thus showed that their love of senseless frolic was stronger than their reverence for the house of prayer.

Long had the good vicar of ancient St. Martin's—the Rev. George Feachem—held the sacred office. He was permitted, on the laying of the foundation stone of the edifice to take its place, to offer a prayer that no blood might be shed during the progress of building, an aspiration which was happily fulfilled. The venerable pastor himself, however, had gone to his rest ere the new edifice was completed. The induction of his successor—the Rev. James Joyce—and the opening of the new building, claim only a passing notice, as both events occurred at a period more recent than the range of these "Recollections." Little did those think who contributed so liberally, and laboured so assiduously towards the erection of the new, but what is now designated the old church, that in less than forty years after its completion, this, in its turn, would give place to a newer one.

THE OLD PLACES OF WORSHIP.

The Friends' or Quakers' Old Meeting House.—The Old Independent "Meeting." — The Holmwood Calvinistic Chapel.

The Friends', or as it was called, Quakers' Old Meeting House, is, as already stated, standing at the rear of some houses at the top of West street. Little more than the shell of the old building, however, remains. The front exterior is altogether changed, and the open space once intervening between it and the street is now covered by the dwellings referred to. Fifty years ago there was a grass plat in front of the Meeting House, and by the wall then skirting the street footpath grew a number of neatly-trimmed trees. The entrance to the enclosure was by a gateway, approached by one or two steps, and a path stretched then across the plat to the porch of the Meeting House. It is said that the building was originally designed for a dwelling-house, and certainly there was but little in its architecture to indicate its being a place of worship. Still the characteristics described, and the date of erection (1709) inscribed on an oval white board just beneath the eaves of the roof, conveyed the idea that the structure was a place of public assemblage. It had in fact about its appearance and surroundings an air of comfort and quietude, strikingly in unison with that of Friends' Meeting Houses in general. A portion of the building was appropriated as a residence for the Meeting House keeper. In that used as the place of meeting, the arrangements were of the simplest character, for they consisted chiefly of a platform and seats, and a moveable screen separating, when required, the men's and women's meetings. It was in this unpretentious building that the Friends had for generations met, through good and through evil report, for devout, yet usually silent worship. Half a century ago the dress of the worshippers, unlike that of many of the junior members of the society in the present day, was almost without exception that of the early Friends, indeed such a laxity of apparel as is now permitted would not at that time have been tolerated for a moment by the seniors in sober homely drab. Sometimes then as now, the ordinarily silent service would give place to, or be supplemented by one to which the public generally would be invited. It was on one of these special occasions, fifty-three years ago, that the eminent Joseph John

Gurney preached, and so great was the desire to hear him, that not only that part of the building generally used for worship, but that appropriated to domestic purposes also, and a tent erected outside, were thoroughly filled. The service was proceeding, when all of a sudden one side of the floor in the domestic part of the building gave way, and precipitated about sixty of those present into the cellar below. Foremost amongst these was a fishmonger of corpulent proportions, who, on finding the floor giving way, firmly grasped the coat tails of a neighbour in front of him. This act, however, failed to save him, and down he went, and the tails with him, to the region below. "Stop! stop!" cried the fishmonger, to those who were following his example. " I wish we could," was the only response our lusty friend received from one who perhaps was by no means sorry to have a substance less hard than *terra firma* to alight upon. Happily there was no loss of life from the accident, although of course a few bruises and no little fright to those who were present, were its natural results. Mr. Gurney's calmness and earnestness were strikingly exemplified on the occasion, for as soon as the confusion was over he resumed his address to those who yet remained in the uninjured part of the building. The cause of the accident was found to have been the rotting of the floor joists by a drain immediately near; the moral of it unquestionably is, that attention, more perhaps than is generally given, ought to be paid ordinarily, and more particularly so on extraordinary occasions, to the stability of places of public assemblage. It was not till many years after this occurred that the Friends left their old meeting house for a new, more commodious, and more pleasantly-situated one on Rose Hill.

The other old Meeting House, or as it was usually called, " Meeting " in West Street, occupied a part of the site of the present Independent or Congregational place of worship. Its date of erection (1719) was engraven on one of its bricks, which, on the demolition of the old Sanctuary, was transferred to the present one. When I first remember it—now more than fifty years ago—it was in the possession of the Independents, and had been then indeed for about a dozen years. The tradition was then extant, however, that during the last century the old Meeting House was Presbyterian, and there are various reasons which might be urged for its correctness. An old gentleman of the name of Weller, whose palsied chin made him an object of general commiseration, had the reputation of having once been one of the Presbyterian elders, and I have heard the names of two others who had held the same office. It is stated that when the old structure passed into the hands of the Independents the state of affairs was most deplorable, for the congregation is said to have dwindled down to three persons, one of them the grandfather of one of the attendants at the present place of worship. The well remembered old Meeting House was approached by a rather narrow passage, which ultimately branched off to the two front doors of the building. At the entrance of this passage, on the left hand, there then stood an old-fashioned dwelling-house, having an air of homeliness and comfort about it. This was the residence of an eminently excellent lady, named Alexander, whose hospitality and kindliness, especially in the entertainment of Christian ministers, was well-known both far and near. On the demolition of the Meeting House, this old dwelling was also pulled down, and its site, or the larger portion of it, appropriated to purposes of burial. The adjoining residence was at the same time greatly improved.

The Meeting House was of red brick, and the roof of pan-tiles. This latter circumstance led to the attendants being sometimes vulgarly designated "pan-tilers." In addition to this they were called "meetingers" and "Methodists," and the service was disturbed in bygone years by the flight of birds, which were wilfully let loose to annoy the preacher and his hearers. Happily such gross displays of malignity and folly are now all but unknown. It is gratifying, too, that in these days of religious liberty, popular opinion and the shield of the law are in accord in maintaining the rights of conscience and the freedom of worship. The interior of the old building was of a quaint description. Around it, except on the side where the pulpit stood, were heavy-looking galleries, painted drab. The pulpit was of the same colour, and of a wine-glass shape. On either side of it was a large circular-headed window, which admitted an abundance of light, and gave to the place an aspect of cheeriness which it would not have otherwise possessed. In front of the pulpit was the table pew, where the choir were stationed, and whose instruments usually consisted of a clarionet, a bassoon, and, if I remember aright, sometimes also of a flute and a bass-viol. At a later period a clarionet only was used. The singing of fifty years ago, though not characterised by the exact technical rendering of that of the present day, had about it a heartiness which, there is cause for regret, is too often absent now. Half a century ago Dorking had no gas, and this old place of worship was lighted by candles in chandeliers suspended from the ceiling, and often has the interest of the juveniles been awakened to see the worthy female meeting-house keeper go through the operation of snuffing and sometimes extinguishing, and then re-lighting the candles. The first sermon on behalf of Christian Missions that I ever remember hearing in the Old Meeting House, now long, long ago, was by a good missionary named Wray, who related during his discourse that a little boy in one of the mission schools had said spontaneously of his still heathen father's idol, certainly with some 'cuteness as well as Christian enlightenment :—

"My father's god 's a great block of wood,
He isn't any harm, nor yet any good."

The Sunday School, the oldest in the parish, and one of the oldest in the county, was well attended. Its funds, at the period referred to, were contributed to by some of the neighbouring gentry, and so abundant was the amount subscribed that the scholars were clothed, as well as instructed. The sight was an interesting one, long to be remembered, when the girls in white tippets and straw bonnets—real unmistakable bonnets—and the boys in corduroy, blending their sweet voices, and led by the dulcet notes of the flute, sang their hymn of praise on anniversary days. The minister, rather more than fifty years ago, was the Rev. John Whitehouse, a saintly man, who was much beloved, and who died at an early age, and to him succeeded the Rev. Alfred Dawson, who, although he, like the good old vicar, assisted in originating a new place of worship for his flock, like him also was prevented by sickness and death from preaching in the new edifice. The foundation stone of the new Chapel—the old designation Meeting House being thenceforward discarded—was laid September 3rd, 1834. I well remember the ceremony and the service with which it was associated. Not the least appropriate part of the latter was the singing of the beautiful Psalm commencing thus :—

From all that dwell below the skies,
Let the Creator's praise arise ;
Let the Redeemer's Name be sung,
In every land, by every tongue.

A brass plate and some coins of the realm were deposited in the stone ; the former with an inscription narrating that " a congregation of Protestant Dissenters had existed in Dorking from the year 1662," and giving a brief history of the old place of worship, of the circumstances which led to the erection of a new one, and of the events of the day.

It now only remains to be stated that the small Calvinistic Meeting House or Chapel on the Holmwood, looked much the same forty or fifty years ago, and, I believe, had then a congregation of about the same size as when it was recently superseded by a new place of worship.

THE OLD SCHOOLS.

TWO COPYBOOKS OF A HUNDRED YEARS AGO.—THE PUBLIC AND PRIVATE SCHOOLS OF THE TOWN.—The HAPLESS SCHOOLMASTER.

It is needless to remark that in Dorking, and throughout the country generally, the state of education, both in regard to its character and diffusion, was very different fifty years ago from what it is now. Were we to go back another half century, the contrast between the past and the present would be still greater. Perhaps, however, the popular idea now extant as to the past might with some justice be a little modified. I have now before me, for instance, two old copybooks, once belonging to the son of a yeoman, one of which bears the date, March 1st, 1774, and the other, February 6th, 1776, or rather more than a hundred years ago.

The writing in these old documents shows most conclusively that, in this department of education, the standard was by no means a low one. In fact, the penmanship throughout the books is equal to that of the pupils of to-day. There is so much in and about these old documents that is curious and suggestive, that a description of them may not be uninteresting. In size they are smaller than the copybooks of the present day, and, in appearance, are decidedly inferior. On the cover of one of them is a roughly executed woodcut, designed to represent "Admiral Vernon's Fleet bombarding Cartagena;" on that of the other, a symbolical representation of the moon. Interspersed throughout both the books are text copies, forms of receipts, and promissory notes; while, in that of the later date, are models of epistolary correspondence. It is in the last named, and in the text copies, however, that there is most to interest and amuse. A considerable proportion of the copies are in quaintly expressed rhyme. Here are some of them :—" By delight, and some care, we come to write fair." "A lad that would excel, must mind his copy well." "Honour and renown, will the ingenious crown." "Put to your tongue a bridle, that it talk not idle." "Neither too silent be, nor talk too free." "Noise and talk without some rule, doth indicate the man a fool." "Evil men and sly, take care how you come nigh." "Good manners in a lad, will make his parents glad." "Good manners, grace, and truth, are ornaments in youth." "Virtue all commend, but few do it attend." "Time passeth away, no mortal can make it stay."

The models of letter writing are highly suggestive. They contribute not a little material, indeed, by which to judge in what light the filial, and other relationships of life were then regarded. One is struck, on reading these old specimens of correspondence, with the contrast between the veneration towards parents, and other relatives, inculcated at that time, and the want of due respect to them sometimes complained of in the present day. Here is a model letter, from a nephew to his uncle :—

"HONOURED UNCLE,
"Not hearing from you in such a length of time, as from the 11th of June last, I am concerned lest sickness, or some accident, hath happened to you, or to some of your family. My uneasiness occasions me giving you this trouble, and I wish that I may find things with you better than my fears suggest. However, be pleased to let me know the certainty with all convenient speed, and thereby you'll very much oblige, Sir,
"Your real Friend,
"And very humble Servant,
"Feb. 28th, 1776." "JOHN SADLER.

The following is a fanciful epistle from a daughter to her father, on an event of peculiar interest. The clever way in which the young lady is made to treat the subject; seeking to know her parent's opinion and wishes, and, adroitly revealing her own, is highly amusing :—

"HONOURED SIR,
"As young Mr. Smith, whose father I am sensible is one of your intimate acquaintance, has, during your absence in the country, made an open declaration of his passion for me, and prest me closely to comply with his over-

tures of marriage, I thought it my duty to decline all offers of that nature, however advantageous they might seem to be, till I had your thoughts on so important an affair; and I am absolutely determined, either to discourage his addresses, or to keep him, at least, in suspense, till your return, as I shall be directed by your superior judgment. I beg leave, however, with due submission, to acquaint you of the idea I have entertained of him, and hope I am not too blind, or partial, in his favour. He seems to me to be perfectly honourable in his intentions, and to be no ways inferior to any gentleman of my acquaintance, either in regard to good sense, or good manners. I frankly own, sir, I could admit of his addresses with pleasure, were they attended with your consent and approbation. Be assured, however, that I am not so far engaged as to act with precipitation, or comply with any offers, inconsistent with that filial duty which, in gratitude to your paternal indulgence, I shall ever owe you. Your speedy instruction, therefore, in so momentous an article, will prove the greatest satisfaction imaginable to,

"Honoured Sir, your most dutiful Daughter,
"March 12th, 1776."   "NANNY PUTTOCK."

Another model letter, in this instance assumed to be addressed by a sailor abroad to his sweetheart at home, is so characteristic, and so truly amusing, that, somewhat long though it be, I am tempted to give it. Here it is:—

"MY DEAR PEGGY,

"If you think of me half so often as I do of you, it will be every hour, for you are never out of my thoughts; and, when I am asleep, I constantly dream of my dear Peggy. I wear my half bit of gold always at my heart, tied to a blue ribbon round my neck, for true blue, my dearest love, is a colour of colours to me. Where, my dearest, do you put yours? I hope you are careful of it, for it would be a bad omen to lose it.

"I hope you hold in the same mind still, my dearest dear, for God will never bless you if you break the vows you have made to me. As to your ever faithful William, I would sooner have my heart torn from my breast, than it should harbour a wish for any other woman besides my Peggy. O, my dearest love! you are the joy of my life! My thoughts are all of you; you are with me in all I do, and my hopes and my wishes are only to be yours. God send it may be so!

"Our Captain talks of sailing soon for England, and then, and then, my dearest Peggy! O how I rejoice, how my heart beats with delight, that makes me I cannot tell how, when I think of arriving in England, and joining hands with my Peggy, as we have our hearts before, I hope! I am sure I speak for one. John Arthur, in the good ship 'Elizabeth,' Captain Winterton, which is returning to England, as I hope we shall soon, promises to deliver this into your own dear hand, and he will bring you too six bottles of citron water, as a token of my love. It is fit for the finest lady's taste; it is so good, and is, what they say, ladies drink—when they can get it.

"John says he will have one sweet kiss of my dearest Peggy, for his care and pains. So let him, my best love, for I am not of a jealous temper. I have a better opinion of my dearest than so. But oh! that I was in his place! One kiss should not serve my turn, tho' I hope it may his—yet, if he takes two, I'll forgive him, one for me and one for himself, for I love John dearly; and so you may well think. Well, what shall I say more! or, rather, what shall I say next! for I have an hundred things crowding in upon me when I write to my dearest; and, alas, one has so few opportunities! but yet I must leave off, for I have written to the bottom of my paper. Love then to all friends, and duty to both our mothers, conclude me,

"Your faithful lover till death,
"WILLM. LAMPORT.

"February 9th, 1776."

However favourable the impression produced by these interesting old copy-books may be, it must be remembered that they are those of a better middle-class school. They give no clue, therefore, to the state of education a century ago among the masses. That among the latter at this period, and even fifty years later, there was generally a lack of the rudiments of learning is certain, and especially so in the villages and country districts throughout the land. For instance, it is said that so dense was the ignorance among the peasantry in a village west of Dorking fifty, or even forty years ago, that they were unacquainted with the names of the days of the week. Thus, it is said that they knew Sunday as "Church-going day," Monday, as "The day after Church-going day," Tuesday, as "Father's hog-killing day," Wednesday, as "The day before Darking Day" (or Dorking Market day), Thursday, as "Darking day," Friday, as "The day after Darking day," and Saturday, as "The day before Church-going day." It is only just to remark, however, that chiefly through the kind liberality of the principal landowner of the parish referred to, such a state of things no longer exists.

I will now describe the educational establishments in Dorking from forty to fifty years ago. They were of the character of those of the period in general. Of the public scholastic institutions there were the National Schools in the Mint, the oldest of the kind in the parish, and of which for many years Mr. and Mrs. Ceaton were the master and mistress. Then there was the Infant School, in East Street, conducted for a long period by Mr. and Mrs. Patching. Churchmen and Dissenters for a series of years united in their support of this last-named school, and it is much to be regretted that at last a spirit of ecclesiastical rivalry brought about its dissolution. More recent in date were the Royal British Schools, the girls' branch of which was commenced in a house at the top of West Street, about forty years ago, Miss Evans being the first mistress. This was followed by the appropriation of the present schoolhouse in Back Lane and the opening of the boys' school under Mr. Bingham. In addition to these public day schools there were the Sunday schools of the Parish Church, which were of a later date than the National Schools—and, as already described, the Sunday School of the Independents.

The private educational establishments of half a century ago, included a number of what are now called Dame Schools. Whatever might have been said of the educational standard of the "governesses"—for such the mistresses of these schools were called—they were, at any rate in Dorking, truly kind-hearted persons, and generously considerate in the exercise of their vocation. So favourable, indeed, was the opinion entertained of the proprietors of these unpretentious establishments, that to them was confided the preparatory education of the sons and daughters of the tradespeople in general. One of the favourite employments of the pupils of these establishments, and indeed of seminaries of a higher standard at that time, was the working of "samplers," a homely occupation, but a useful one, for it taught the scholar the art of marking. The "sampler" was much prized also in after years as a memorial of the pupil's attainments. Then, too, there was the making of patchwork quilts, in which the little boys as well as the female scholars in the Dame Schools were sometimes employed. The Ladies' Seminaries of forty and fifty years ago are not now surpassed or even equalled in Dorking, either in regard to the number of the establishments or of their scholars. There is no Ladies' Boarding School in the place now that can vie in numbers with the large and prosperous seminary so long conducted by the Misses Stent and Sumner in South Street. During that period, too, there were the educational establishments of the Misses Eives and Brewer, of Miss Andrews, of Miss Agar, of Miss Gilliam (the late Mrs. Lanham), and of the Misses White and Beckett.

One of the oldest and most flourishing boys' schools of half a century or more ago was that of Mr. Lansdell, in West Street. To this school most of the tradesmen's sons of the town were sent. A custom then existed, not only at this establishment, but in schools of the same class generally, which has now, I believe, long fallen into disuse. I refer to the writing of " Christmas pieces," a usage designated to exhibit the progress made by the pupil in penmanship during the year. It may not be uninteresting to give a description of these things of the past. The " Christmas Piece " of fifty years ago was a broad sheet with a woodcut painted in gaudy colours at the top of it, illustrative of some sacred or secular subject. On either side of the sheet were smaller pictures, with the same design, while in the middle a blank space was left for a specimen of the pupil's writing, and at the bottom of the sheet an encircled tablet for his name and the date of the piece. The first piece of which I have a vivid remembrance illustrated a Christmas of the olden period, in which the dancing and music, the sliding and skating, and the good things of the season—not forgetting a bonny plum pudding and a large iced and otherwise ornamented twelfth cake—were duly represented. I remember also pieces with sacred subjects, such as " Joseph's dream," " Moses and the burning bush," and " Daniel in the lion's den." At that time, perhaps more than now, much was thought of a good handwriting, and no little anxiety was manifested to produce on these occasions the very best specimens of penmanship. Sometimes, by way of giving a finishing touch, the master would supplement the exploit of the pupil by garnishing what had been written with sundry and divers cunningly-executed flourishes. Steel pens were then not invented, and much of the master's time in the morning was taken up by mending the goose-quill pens then in use, the scholars applying to him for "a large hand," "a text hand," "a round hand," or "a small hand," as the case might require. Mr. Lansdell's preference for land measuring led to his relinquishment of the school, which, however, was not so flourishing in the hands of his successor. Another middle-class boys' school, but at a slightly later period, was that of Mr. John Worsfold, and a third, and well attended one, was commenced about five-and-forty years ago, and conducted long afterwards by Mr. Henry Lanham. Contemporaneous with Mr. Lansdell's school was one at Westcott, some of the scholars of which were from Dorking. This establishment belonged to a little old-fashioned gentleman of somewhat odd appearance and habits. I well remember the little man, dressed in a drab-coloured coat, extending almost to his heels, knee breeches, and broad-brimmed hat riding on his donkey into Dorking, and looking every inch of him like a schoolmaster of the olden time. Many and curious were the stories once afloat respecting the old master. On one occasion it is stated he remarked—it would seem by way of magnifying his office—" I *eddecated* those two gentlemen going up the street." At another time, as the story goes, he was asked by two other gentlemen to be the arbiter in a discussion on the correct spelling of the name of a third. After due consideration, the schoolmaster delivered himself thus: " Well, gentlemen, you see there are no grammar rules for spelling proper names." Of course from this dictum there could be no appeal. Our friend the pedagogue was a firm believer in the efficacy of corporal punishment, and it is said of him that on one occasion, after a free use of the cane, a big unruly Dorking scholar, considerably taller than himself, acting, it would seem, on the proverb that " one good turn deserves another," snatched from the tutor's hand the instrument of correction and tried its effect upon the schoolmaster himself. Bad though this was for the poor little man, I have heard from an eye-witness that after this a sadder calamity befel him. One day, more than five-and-forty years ago, a scholar, either wilfully or innocently, offended the warm-tempered schoolmaster. The other scholars sympathised with their friend in trouble, who was now called upon to beg the master's pardon. This the pupil refused to do, whereupon the instructor's wife was called to hold the refractory boy while her husband gave him a caning. The anger of the other scholars now became ungovernable, and, seizing the master, they bound him hand and foot and carried him off to a large copper, into which they cast him. The lid was immediately put on, and some of the boys sat upon it to keep it down. The hapless schoolmaster cried aloud for mercy, but mercy there was none. Some of the boys now looked about for fuel, and, finding an old grogram gown and one or two aprons, they thrust them into the copper hole and set fire to them, thus giving to their unhappy master what they termed "a good warming." The poor spouse of the tutor was, of course, frantic, and, bursting through the restraint which some of the boys had for a time placed upon her, she ran from the house for assistance. The ringleaders of the movement, seeing the position of affairs, now fled, and the hapless master was soon after this released. Of course, after such an indignity, the little moral influence which the poor schoolmaster had previously possessed was utterly gone. It need hardly be said that the effect upon the school was most disastrous. A gentleman of the neighbourhood, who had kindly paid the fees of twelve of the scholars, at once draughted them off elsewhere, while the parents of a number of pupils besides, without hesitation, transferred their sons to other establishments where, happily, less severity and more discipline prevailed.

THE OLD INSTITUTIONS.

THE MECHANICS' INSTITUTION.—THE PROVIDENT INSTITUTE.—THE BENEFIT CLUBS.

The earliest organisation founded specially for the mental elevation of the operative classes that I remember in Dorking was the Mechanics' Institute. Its reading-room was within the precincts of the old Queen's Arms in West Street, and its lectures were usually delivered at the old infant schoolroom in East Street. Some of the professional gentlemen and other influential inhabitants of the town took great interest in the welfare of the institution, and for a time it progressed satisfactorily. It was subsequently thought that it would succeed still better by receiving a more pretentious title, hence it was called afterwards the Literary and Scientific Institute. Lectures, characterised by considerable ability, were delivered by gentlemen in the neighbourhood, and by others from a distance. Among those of the former were one or two of a clever and highly interesting character on the structure and functions of the human eye, by the late Mr. W. Chaldecott.

Ultimately the interest that was at first manifested in the institution declined, and at last it was given up.

In succeeding years a Mutual Improvement Society was started, but this organisation was a short-lived one. Then the original Young Men's Christian Association was founded, and after its extinction arose the Working Men's Institute, but these two organisations were commenced at a period later than the range of these "Recollections." It may be said, however, respecting the last-named excellent institution, that it has now had a longer existence than any previous one of the kind in Dorking.

The Provident Institution is an organisation with a different object from the societies just referred to, for, as its name expresses, it seeks to encourage among the industrious classes the spirit and practice of frugality and providence. This it does by supplying flour and coals in the winter at a price lower than the ordinary retail charge, adding at the same time a percentage to the amount subscribed by the members during the other parts of the year. Mr. Timbs, in 1822, quoted from the fifth annual report of the institution, so that it has now existed for about sixty years. He then said of it —" It ought not to be forgotten that during five years upwards of *twelve hundred pounds* have been raised by public subscription for the support of the fund, and that the contributions of the poor subscribers have been proportionately important." One is glad to hear, at so early a period in its existence, an account like this of this commendable society, and the inhabitants of Dorking may well be proud to know that " Provident Institutions took their rise in this congenial soil." They may think, perhaps, that the importance of the Dorking Provident Institution is a little over-estimated when it is stated in the fifth report that it " may fearlessly be held up as a grand and practical scheme for the social and moral improvement of mankind." Still it may be said of the institution in sober truthfulness that during its long and honourable career it has done a good work, has been ably conducted, and has deserved, and still deserves, the support of the benevolent.

The old Benefit Club, or Friendly Society, was, before the rise of its more recent competitors—the Odd Fellows', Foresters', and Good Templars' organisations—a popular and flourishing institution in Dorking. Imperfect though the constitution of the old Friendly Society was, and objectionable though some of its usages were, it was at least a step in the right direction, for it encouraged among its members the spirit of self-reliance and of a manly independence—the very backbone of the nation's strength—and helped to stem the tide of a wide-spread pauperism which at one time threatened to sap the very foundation of the country's prosperity.

The oldest Benefit Club in Dorking fifty years ago was the "Surrey Yeoman." This club was originated in May, 1799, at the old Star, in West Street, and was afterwards transferred to the inn first named. For many years, I believe, it was the only friendly society in the neighbourhood. At the Yeoman it flourished to such an extent that at one period it numbered more than 400 members. Its feast day was on Whit-Monday, a high day and holiday, not only for its members, but for the wives and daughters of the married, and the sweethearts of the unmarried, clubmen. On this day, headed by the Dorking band and the banners of the club, the members, decked with blue favours, walked in procession to church. One of the flag-bearers for many years in succession was a stout brewer's drayman, and on either side, as if to guard the faded old banner—dating soon after the foundation of the society—were some of the veteran fathers of the club—one a portly blacksmith, with a huge nosegay in his coat button-hole, from Westcott, and another known by everybody in the neighbourhood as "Old Billy Waters," and who lived in hale health to a green old age far beyond the allotted span of threescore years and ten. The service at church being over, the procession was re-formed, and after parading the streets, the members retired to dine. The old club passed through a number of changes. First, there was a secession from it, and a number of its members formed a new society at the Ram Inn. Then, in course of time, its members still further diminished, and it was subsequently transferred to the Queen's Head Inn. Here it lingered on almost in obscurity, for the glories of its feast day were no longer visible, and ceased to exist four or five years ago.

The Ram Club, formed on the secession from the Surrey Yeoman, afterwards suffered from the same cause, for a number of the members left it and started a new society at the Queen's Head, which was thenceforth known as the Queen's Head Club. The society that was still held at the Ram became ultimately transformed into a club of a higher class, and received as its members tradesmen and artisans, and this is its character at the present day.

The Queen's Head Club—an offshoot, as already stated, of the original Ram Club—existed for some years. Its "feast day" was on Easter Monday, when its members, decked with purple and orange favours, a banner of the same colours, and a band of music, attended church and paraded the streets.

The Three Tuns Club is a Society which has now existed for a long period. Its members, like those of the Ram, dispense with an attendance at church and a procession through the streets on the feast day.

The Friendly Society at the Norfolk Arms, in the Holmwood, must have existed now almost, or quite forty years. It has the same procession and attendance at church once incident to the older clubs.

In later years another club has sprung into existence also on the Holmwood, its head-quarters being at the "Holly and Laurel." It was established, however, at too recent a period to claim here more than a passing notice.

Another and an older Friendly Society, although more distant from the town, demands from us more than a mere recognition. I refer to the old and once popular club at Ockley. Half a century ago, Ockley Club vied with any institution of the kind, whether far or near; in fact, few, if any, of the Friendly Societies of the border towns of Surrey and Sussex had so many hundred members as this village club, many of whom resided in Dorking and the neighbourhood around. The concomitants of Ockley Club day were like those of a large fair. Crowds of holiday makers from our own town, and even from places more distant, were present on the occasion, and met on the village green—a spot where tradition says a mole hill never rises, because of the blood once shed here in mortal combat between the English and the Danes.

We mention this tradition, although it may be as baseless as another, which says of the same spot that it was here, in centuries past, that the inhabitants intended to build the parish church, but that the fairies removed by night the materials deposited here in the day, to the distant spot where the church now stands. It is said, moreover, that so invincible was the pertinacity of these marvellous beings, that the original idea had to be abandoned, and the present site of the edifice adopted.

It is much to be regretted that the old club festival day,

instead of being one of innocent recreation and rational enjoyment, was too frequently marred by a debasing intemperance. It is equally to be deplored, also, that through the faulty basis and imperfect working of these well-intentioned societies, and their consequent final collapse, many a hardworking man who, in the prime of his days, had paid the member's fee for relief in sickness, has found himself in old age with health gone, hopes blighted, and the cold shade of pauperism and the Union House before him. Happily the legally enforced sounder basis of the New Friendly Society, and the guaranteed Government security of the Post-office Annuity have now rendered so sad an ending of industrial life more avoidable, if not entirely so.

Even yet, however, something more might be wisely done, whereby the industrial classes could, by an investment of their savings, secure for themselves a more ample provision to sustain and comfort them in their declining years.

THE OLD INSTITUTIONS.

THE HORTICULTURAL SOCIETY.—COTTAGERS' SHOW.—AGRICULTURAL ASSOCIATION.—CHRISTMAS STOCK AND POULTRY SHOWS.—ARCHERY MEETINGS.—SAVINGS BANK.—THE OLD PRIVATE BANKS.

Forty, or five and forty years ago, Dorking possessed a flourishing Horticultural Society. Its exhibitions were a credit to the neighbourhood, for at them were shown an abundance of fruit and vegetables of the finest varieties and culture, and flowers of the newest and choicest descriptions. Generally speaking, indeed, the products exhibited were of superior excellence, but this was especially the case among those fruits and flowers which evoked a spirited competition. Among the former were pine apples, grapes, melons, and other table fruit, and among the latter, the cactus, rose, camellia, pink, dahlia, pansy, and the auricula. The exhibition drew together a large number of admiring spectators, and at one time it seemed as if the Dorking Horticultural Society would become a permanent institution, but like the beautiful flowers once exhibited in such profusion on its show days, it ultimately faded and died.

The Cottagers' Show sprang into existence in the days of the Society just described, and continued a useful career long after its contemporary had ceased to be. Its influence was unquestionably a good one, indeed the good the show did can hardly be estimated, for it not only stimulated the culture of fruit, vegetables, and flowers in the cottage garden, and yielded to the successful exhibitor a welcome addition to his limited resources, but it bound the cottager more closely to his home, and without doubt had an elevating and otherwise wholesome influence upon his character. The Cottagers' Show, during its somewhat lengthened existence, owed much of its success to its honorary secretary, Mr. Charles Hart, who held that post efficiently till the cessation of the show, an event which occurred four or five years ago, and which was mainly due to the formation of new exhibitions of the same character in the neighbourhood.

The Dorking Agricultural Association is another defunct institution, which forty years ago, or thereabouts, had its annual ploughing matches, its dinner, and the usual other accessories to an organisation of this kind. At a later period arose the Christmas Stock Show, and this also had a lamentable end.

Happily this does not apply to the Dorking Christmas Poultry show, which still exists, and long, very long, may it flourish, as it certainly ought, in the town that has given a name to one of the most renowned breeds of poultry in the world. All honour, too, to those who have striven, and are striving to maintain the reputation of Dorking by rearing in its neighbourhood its breed of "five-claws."

The Archery Meetings, supported so zealously forty years ago by Lady Elizabeth Wathen, and held sometimes in the meadow facing Shrub Hill, and at others in Betchworth Park, are now events of the past.

One of the oldest institutions in Dorking which yet exists, is the Savings Bank. This commendable organisation has, during its long career, done an excellent service by offering to the industrious a safe deposit for their savings. This was a boon which was all the more valuable during the instability of banks of issue, and before the institution of the Post-office Savings Bank. I am not aware in what year the old Savings Bank was established, but as it is mentioned in the *Promenade Round Dorking*, published in 1822, it must have had an existence of more than half a century.

Another old institution in Dorking was the Private Bank. An establishment of the kind located in the house now occupied by Mr. John Maybank, adjoining the Wheatsheaf Inn, had collapsed before I remember. Rather more than fifty years ago there were two others, those of Messrs. Piper and Dewdney, and of Messrs. Piper, Gale, Nash and Neale. The business of the first was conducted in the residence occupied by Mr. Rossiter, in High Street, and of the last-named in that now tenanted by Mr. Playfoot, just opposite. All three of the banks named were banks of issue; one-pound notes constituting a large part of their "circulation." At that period, in fact, no inconsiderable portion of the floating capital of the country consisted of the notes of the private banker, and this circumstance led too frequently to an anxiety and a loss from which the public is now happily exempted. A bank panic at that time was indeed a serious matter, for it brought not only ruin to the bank, but insolvency to the tradesman, and what was as sad as either, in some cases an almost entire loss of the little all of the hard-working humble investor, or holder of notes. The stoppage of a bank fifty years ago produced a perfect consternation in the locality where it occurred, and tested to the utmost the stability and resources of the neighbouring establishments for a "run" upon them at once commenced. Notwithstanding the friendly aid which was usually accorded under the circumstances, the failure of one bank was too often followed by that of another, thus increasing the loss and suffering already occasioned, and still further shaking the confidence of the public. The establishment of Messrs. Piper and Dewdney was regarded as, and called the Dorking Bank, for here was its chief office, and here, too, resided its proprietors, while the other establishment was but a branch of the Reigate Bank. The bank notes of Messrs. Piper, Gale, Nash, and Neale had for their heading, "Reigate, Croydon, and Darking Bank;" this mode of spelling the name of our town, however, was, as already pointed out, an incorrect one. If I mistake not it was the Bank Panic of 1825 that proved too severe a strain upon the establishment of Messrs. Piper and Dewdney; but on realising their respective assets, the estate of the latter was found to have been almost, if not entirely, solvent. The failure of Messrs. Piper and Dewdney's Bank caused a tremendous "run" on that of Messrs. Piper, Gale, Nash, and Neale, who the more conveniently to meet the demands upon them, and to aid in restoring confidence, for some days opened their establishment an hour earlier, and closed it an hour later than usual. So severe was the pressure upon the Bank that seven-eighths of its notes were paid in. Yet it passed through the crisis unscathed, and, of course, after such an ordeal confidence in it was the reverse of diminished. Subsequently the last-named firm was reconstructed; the third and fourth partners only thenceforth constituting it. From this time till the starting of a branch of the London and County Bank—now about forty years ago—Messrs. Nash and Neale's was the only banking establishment in Dorking. After an interval of some years, this last private bank in the town collapsed, but with so handsome a dividend as to demonstrate that its stoppage might, under ordinary circumstances, have been averted. I must not close this notice of the old private banks in Dorking without narrating one or two incidents connected with their history. I have been told (for the circumstance was before my remembrance) that early in the century a resident of some position in the neighbourhood was implicated in a transaction which led the proprietors of the Dorking Bank to proceed against him at the County Assizes at Kingston. The trial ended adversely to the individual referred to, and so strong was the popular feeling in favour of the proprietors that the last-named received a public ovation, while the former was burnt in effigy in front of the Red Lion Hotel, the signboard being removed on the occasion, to permit in its place the suspension of the effigy. The other incident was of a very different character, and occurred at a later period. One night an attempt at robbery by burglars was made upon one of the banks. The thieves, in the course of their operations, by a misadventure dropped one of their implements upon the pavement. The noise thus produced alarmed the manager, who, suspecting what was afoot, quickly left his bedroom with a blunderbuss in one hand and a candle in the other, and, thus equipped, descended the stairs. The manager, good man, in his haste, had quitted his sleeping apartment with but little addition to his nocturnal costume, and with his nightly headgear unremoved; and in this attire he searched the house till he reached the basement. The robbers' misadventure had stopped their operations, but they still remained outside to watch the result. No doubt observing the light below, they peeped through the basement grating. The spectacle which thereupon caught their gaze was too much even for a burglar's gravity, for so amused were the thieves at the odd sight before them, that they burst into a loud laugh, and ran hastily off.

THE OLD INSTITUTIONS.

THE CORN, STOCK, AND POULTRY MARKETS.—THE CATTLE AND PLEASURE FAIRS.—PUNCH BOWL FAIR.—THE "FOX" FAIR.

The Corn Market has existed in Dorking for nearly six hundred years. It has been held, since the demolition of the Old Market House, in front of the Three Tuns Inn. Fifty years ago, there was, at the last-named spot, the same gathering on Thursday afternoons as now, the same busy hum of conversation, the same opening of sample bags, and testing of samples; the same racy remark and innocent joke, and sometimes, too, the same driving of a hard bargain. Then, however, as already stated, not a little of the corn that was sold was "pitched" at the Tuns and the Black Horse. Then, too, there were more round frocks, more grey "Newmarket cut" coats, and more top boots than now. In the olden time also the price of wheat and other grain ranged higher than at present, for in these days of free trade it seldom reaches £20, and never £50 the load—the price occasionally, though rarely so in the bad harvest years of the Corn Law times, of from fifty to sixty years ago. And, I fear, it is too true that there are fewer buyers and sellers at the market now than there were then.

The Stock Market was originated just half a century ago. Its establishment was a source of gratification to the tradespeople generally, and to the farmers for miles around, while to the youngsters, who gleefully aided the drovers, it was a cause of delight. For many years the market was well stocked, and as a natural consequence, was well attended by buyers. In its early years, indeed, the horned cattle occupied the south side of High Street, from Chequer Yard to the Red Lion Hotel. The sheep pens, on the same side of the road, stretched from the hotel named to the White Horse Inn, while a similar space was covered on the opposite side of the street by additional pens for sheep and pigs. In fact, according to an old market toll book, which I have recently seen, the pens on some market days exceeded fifty in number. When the Stock Market was first established, and for many years after, it was held on the second Thursday in the month, and while this arrangement continued, both sellers and buyers knew when it would take place, but the fatal mistake was made of holding the market once in four weeks, and from this time it began to decline. Other changes equally unwise were subsequently made, and year after year the market continued to dwindle, till now it may be said no longer to exist. A more effectual mode to bring about its extinction, even if this had been designed, than that adopted, could hardly have been devised.

The Poultry Market, or as it is often called, the Fowl Market, is a very old institution in Dorking. Its origin probably dates back to the same period as that of the Corn Market. When I first remember the Fowl Market, it was very different from what it is now. This market also has deplorably declined. Fifty years ago, the poultry crates extended from opposite the present Post Office to the south of the Bull's Head Inn, and the higglers who attended the market came from a number of the neighbouring towns—a very different state of things to that of the present day. Then it was of common occurrence to see on a Thursday morning the better class cottage housewife trudging along with her crate of fowls slung across her shoulders, the perspiration streaming down her face, and her footsteps bending towards the Market Place. Arrived here, or almost before she reached the spot, there was, when fowls were scarce and dear, such a struggling and bantering between the higglers, and often such high words between them, that a stranger might sometimes wonder how the contention would end, and tremble for the safety both of the fowls and their owner. These were the days, however, that yielded a satisfaction to the worthy housewife, for it was then, when competition was severe, and prices were high, that she was better able to buy the new gown, or some other article of dress; the new teapot, or some other household requisite, or it might be the then dear salt for pickling the porker, or the sugar for the elder wine for Christmas. These were the times, too, when the housewife of another class—the farmer's wife—and her daughters were not above the employment of cramming the capons, of working in the dairy, and of riding on horseback, sometimes with the fowl basket on either side, to market. Then, as now, a special day was usually appointed for the Christmas Poultry Market, the supply at which of capons of prodigious size, of other fowls, of geese, was far superior to what it is now.

The decline of our markets is not merely a matter for regret, but for the prompt and serious consideration of the townspeople in general. Unquestionably the welfare of the town, and especially of its trading population, is intimately associated with a revived prosperity of its markets, and the sooner steps are taken to bring about so desirable a consummation, or, at least, to attempt it, the better.

The Annual Cattle Fair is as old as the Corn Market, and was more flourishing half a century ago than it has been of late years. At the first-named period, I remember seeing the Fair extend from near the present Post-office in the west, to beyond the Surrey Yeoman Inn in the east; the supply of sheep at that time being so great that the pens on the north side of the street stretched from the Red Lion Hotel to opposite the Ram Inn. Fair-day then was thought much more of, in the way of hospitality and the reception of country cousins, than it is now.

The Pleasure Fair, too, was at that time in its prosperous days, both as to the number of its stalls, or, as they were then called, "standings," its shows, its other amusements, and its visitors. It was almost fifty years ago when for one year only the Fair was held on Cotmandene. In the following one, however, it was held again in the town.

Punch Bowl Fair, half a century ago, was a favourite resort for the juveniles of all classes. Early in the afternoon of Easter Monday, the road leading from the town to the Punch Bowl was thronged with groups of well-dressed, as well as more humbly clad children, wending their way to the Fair. How many changes have occurred, how many shadows on the path have fallen, since the then young eyes of the seniors of to-day, glistened with delight at the " fairings " before them! Then how the young hearts beat at a quicker pace, those of the girls at the spectacle of splendid dolls, of gilded crowns, and of brilliant watches, made ready to go—when they were carried! and those of the boys, too, at the sight of painted horses, of playing trumpets, and merry whistlepipes! How, too, the mouths of both boys and girls watered on seeing the piles of gingerbread nuts, oranges, and other delicious things! Innocent were these delights of childhood in the afternoon, but we fear that this can hardly be said of some of the pastimes of the children of larger growth later in the day.

There was another fair which was then held at a farther distance from the town—that of the " Fox " on Ranmore Common. This was called a Cherry Fair, and the day for holding it was on the last Sunday in July. I have heard nothing about it for some years, and it is by no means a cause for regret, if it is held no longer, for of all days in the week, that chosen for this yearly gathering of mirth makers, was the most inappropriate and unjustifiable. I will only add that Leatherhead Fair, which, fifty years ago, was a very popular one, received at that time an accession of visitors from Dorking, and that at the Fair some of the aristocratic ladies of the neighbourhood had stalls for the sale of fancy articles and needlework.

THE OLD COACHES.

BROAD'S COACH.—MR. BROAD, THE SUPPOSED ORIGINAL OF MR. TONY WELLER, THE FATHER OF THE RENOWNED SAM.

Travelling from Dorking to London at the close of the last century strikingly contrasted with the travelling of to-day. The Messrs. Hart had, if they have not now, in their possession, an old coach time-bill of the period first named, in which the announcement was made that the Dorking coach would start from the town to London on one day and return on the next. The same journey can now be accomplished by rail in two hours. I have heard my seniors say that when the journey was first performed in the same day, it was thought an astonishing feat. Even then, through the badness of the roads, the pace was a jogging one, and afforded a full opportunity, not only of viewing the scenery, but for the observation of men and things in general. As time went on, however, matters improved, and at last a speed of slightly exceeding eight miles an hour was attained; for the journey to London, including the time occupied in changing the horses, was accomplished in three hours. I have been told that one of the coaches, in the early part of the century, was driven by a Mr. Shaw. A little later than this, a spirited competition in coaching arose, and was carried on for some time. The competitors were Mr. Thomas Curtis, Mr. Matthew Holden, and Messrs. Chitty and Walker. Mr. Walker afterwards retired from the partnership, and Mr. Chitty was then joined by Mr. Thomas Wright. The departure and arrival of the coach of Mr. Curtis was announced by the notes of a bugle, and this circumstance, in all probability, led the boys of the period to espouse his cause. The coming in of the coaches in the evening gave them a special opportunity of demonstrating their partisanship, and this they did gleefully, by shouting the following lines :—

> "Chitty's horses will not trot,
> Because they get no corn;
> But Curtis he comes galloping in,
> Blowing his bugle horn."

Of course, the statement in the first two lines was more playful than correct, for Chitty's horses, without doubt, did get some corn, or would have quickly failed in their work. To such an extent was the opposition of the rival coaches carried, that two passengers are said to have been taken to London for eighteenpence, or one-third of the ordinary fare for one. It is not surprising that, under such circumstances, a considerable sum of money was lost by the respective proprietors, who were ultimately tired of their worse than profitless competition. Messrs. Chitty and Wright engaged as coachman, towards the close of their proprietorship, a young man who was afterwards a conspicuous character in Dorking, even if he were not the original of one of the prominent figures in a world-renowned novel. I refer to Mr. William Broad who, before his appearance as coachman in our town, was engaged as a postboy at Reigate. While thus employed he paid especial attention to his personal appearance, and adorned his jacket with a row or two of large silver buttons. Then, too, it seems he had often good "jobs," which brought him large earnings. Messrs. Chitty and Wright's coach flourished so much under the coachmanship of Mr. Broad, that he soon became its proprietor. This was a little more than fifty years ago. Broad's coach, as already intimated, started from Dorking at seven in the morning and returned at the same hour in the evening. Its first stage was from here to the King's Head at Epsom, its next to the Angel at Tooting, its last thence to its destination at the Spread Eagle, in Gracechurch Street. It was the coach of the London banker and merchant resident in the neighbourhood, and of the tradesmen of the town generally. It was noted for its general punctuality and the civility of its proprietor, who prided himself not a little on his team, and especially in the four greys with which he horsed his coach from Dorking to Epsom. The fare to London by Broad's coach, and indeed by the other Dorking coaches contemporaneous with his, was five shillings for the outside, and seven shillings for the inside passengers, and of course the same sums respectively for the return journey, and he was thought a shabby passenger who did not add a shilling or so for the coachman. One of the steadiest supporters of Broad's coach was the late Richard

Fuller, Esq., of the Rookery, who might be seen morning by morning occupying the box seat, and who sometimes, in the absence of Mr. Broad, and indeed at others when he was present, would undertake with much affability the duties of coachman. In fact nothing appeared to please Mr. Fuller better, than politely to hand down the coach steps, or catch in his arms, some humbly clad old lady, too stout perhaps to be active, or too timid to be venturesome, receive from her her hearty thanks, the fare, and a small addition for the civil " coachman," all of which were duly acknowledged by an orthodox touch of the hat. That destructionist of the old stagers, the Railroad, proved in the end too powerful a competitor even for the once thriving and popular coach, and it and its belongings submitted to the indignity of a public auction. Mr. Broad—who was familiarly known as "Old Hold Hard"—lived for some years after he left the road, and all that was mortal of him now lies in the Dorking Cemetery, where a grave-stone with the following inscription marks the site of his burial:—

"Sacred
to the memory of
WILLIAM BROAD,
Coach Proprietor for 25 Years in this town,
Who died December 30th, 1862,
Aged 73 Years."

It is interesting to know that an oil colour portrait of Mr. Broad, whip in hand, taken in the later years of his proprietorship, is still in good preservation at his old inn, the Bull's Head.

Coachman Broad has been thought to have been the original of that remarkable character in the Pickwick Papers, Mr. Tony Weller, the father of the renowned Sam, and the landlord of the celebrated Marquis of Granby. Which of the old inns the Marquis was, has been definitively settled by no less an authority than Dickens himself. The readers of "All the Year Round" will remember that in one of a series of articles, entitled "As the crow flies," which appeared in that periodical, September 18th, 1869—less than a year before the great novelist's lamented death—the following interesting statement was made:—

"The crow drops from Ranmore Hill upon Dorking, which stands close to the old Roman Road, or 'Stone Street,' leading from Arundel to the Sussex coast. . . . . The literary pilgrim looks in vain for his special throne—the

Marquis of Granby. The famed house where the fatal widow beguiled old Weller, and where the Shepherd, after imbibing too deeply of his special vanity, was cooled in the horse trough, is gone. Let the pilgrim be informed that the real 'Markis' was the King's Head (now the Post office), a great coaching house on the Brighton Road in the old days, and where many a smoking team drew up when Sammywell was young. Long before old Weller mounted his chariot throne, Dorking was a quiet place, much frequented by London merchants (chiefly the Dutch), who came down to see Box Hill, and to eat fresh-caught perch."

It would, of course, have been additionally interesting if the writer of Pickwick had been equally explicit as to the identity of the Marquis's landlord, for as it is, we are left to what, at best, is mere conjecture. Were Mr. Weller, the elder, copied from an original, it seems pretty evident that the latter was an individual with sharply defined characteristics, or one who in popular language is termed "a character." Such an one was Coachman Broad, in whom, without doubt, the wondrously keen-eyed observer of men and manners would see not a little material to point a moral and adorn a tale. Assuming, however, that Broad were the original of the elder Weller, it must not be supposed for a moment that he possessed all the characteristics ascribed to the old host, or, even those they had in common, to the same grotesque degree. The personal appearance, the domestic relationship, and some of the other circumstances connected with Mr. Broad, were, for instance, not in all respects, if any, like those ascribed to Mr. Tony Weller. The former was not enormously stout, nor did he marry a widow, nor keep an inn. Nor was either of his three sons, as far as I knew them, anything in character like the wayward Sam.

Were Broad, the original of old Weller, it is quite clear that the story of the "Markis" and its characters must have been a compound one of "the old days" and of those more recent. This, however, is by no means unlikely, for novelists, like poets, are allowed, by general consent, a large realm of license. The former, in fact, though aiming to be true to life, are professedly writers of fiction, and as such, embellish the story, or disguise the hero, by adding to the one and ascribing to the other what has happened elsewhere, long before, or what is purely the creation of the novelist's imagination.

Let us see in what respects there was a likeness between the supposed prototype of old Weller and that personage himself. Each was a coachman who "mounted his chariot throne" in Dorking; each was genial, fond of witticisms, and given to smartness in dress. Each was quick tempered, and imperfectly educated. The age of both pretty well agree. Both had the good traits of the old "whips," and both, too, their love of a "special vanity." Of all the old Dorking coachmen, Broad was the likeliest to be appropriated by the master novelist, and if old Weller was copied from either of them, Broad was, in all probability, his original. It may be asked, perhaps, where did Dickens cull the names of the Marquis of Granby and of Weller? The former, probably, from the inn with that sign in the neighbouring town of Epsom, the latter in our own locality. Any one with a moderate acquaintance with Dorking is aware that the name of Weller —a surname, we believe, almost unknown in some parts of the country—is a common one here. There seems a special reason, however, for supposing that the name was derived in our town, for at the time the Pickwick Papers were being written, and when their author was paying visits to Dorking, there was then a young man—now an aged and infirm one— who was hostler to the afternoon coach, and porter to Broad's, who bore this surname. It calls at least for a passing notice, that, at the same period, the White Hart Inn, in the Borough, the old hostelry where the irrepressible Sam first comes into view, was one of the London inns of the chief Dorking carrier. The detestable Stiggins had no prototype then in Dorking, but the horse trough at that time standing outside the Bull's Head Inn, the head-quarters of Broad's coach, and the tradition that some one was once ducked there, might have been suggestive as to the mode of the Shepherd's punishment.

THE OLD COACHES.

Holden's and Walker's Coaches:—The Horsham and other Sussex Coaches.

The second Dorking Morning Coach half a century ago was Holden's, and was driven for some years by its owner, Mr. Matthew Holden, a brother of the well-known Mitcham Coach proprietors. It started at nine o'clock from the Three Tun's Inn, and returned in the evening about six. It was the West-End morning coach, its first stage being from Dorking to Epsom, its second thence to Merton, and its final one from the last-named place to the Golden Cross, Charing Cross. On the death of Mr. Holden, the coach was driven by his eldest son, who bore the same Christian name as his father. An exciting incident occurred in connection with the coach, now almost forty years ago. To the consternation of the residents of the town, it was observed one evening in the Spring to be rapidly passing along the High Street without a driver, and indeed without an outside passenger. The four horses and the vehicle continued their onward and dangerous course till they reached the Potteries in the Holmwood, where they stopped. Inside the coach, during its perilous supplementary journey were Lady and Captain Wathen, and her ladyship's maid, who, with great and commendable presence of mind, kept their seats, and were thus providentially preserved unhurt. The coach and horses, too, were not in the slightest injured. On Mr. Matthew Holden, the younger, becoming the landlord of the Red Lion Hotel, this became the headquarters of the coach, and continued to be so till the railway compelled its withdrawal from the road.

The other Dorking Coach, fifty years ago was an afternoon one, and was driven by Mr. Joseph Walker, its proprietor. It started from the Bull's Head at three o'clock, and after calling at the Three Tuns, proceeded on its first stage to Epsom, thence to Tooting, and on to its destination—the Golden Cross, Charing Cross. It left the last-named great coaching house on the following morning and reached Dorking about noon. Early in the history of the coach, a serious accident befel it. It was stopping, it appears, on its way down at one of the inns at Ewell, when a little child who was sitting just behind the box seat, vigorously, but of course innocently, kicked the coach with his foot. The noise thus produced frightened the horses, which at once started off without the driver, and a collision, which upset the coach, almost immediately afterwards occurred. One poor lady, a Mrs. Bailey, was killed on the spot, or died directly afterwards from the injuries she sustained. Some of the other passengers were seriously hurt, but happily without a fatal result. This sad catastrophe, it is needless to say, produced a profoundly painful sensation in Dorking, and its effect upon Mr. Walker was so disastrous, that it is said he was never thoroughly well afterwards. He continued, however, still to drive the coach, till his health became so shattered that he was at last obliged to relinquish a post he had held for three-and-twenty years. Some time before Mr. Walker's decease, the coach passed into the hands of his brother, Mr. Israel Walker—I believe now the only surviving old Dorking Coach proprietor, and the oldest tradesman in the town—who continued to hold the proprietorship till the coach was taken off the road, now almost forty years ago. The history of this old coach affords a singular illustration of the fluctuation in the "earnings" of the old stagers. It is stated, for instance, in an old "earnings book," a sight of which I have been favoured with, that on several days only a few shillings were received from passengers, and that one day, during "Murphy's Frost," not a single penny was earned. On the other hand, during the Epsom Races week, as much as £80 would be sometimes received for fares.

In addition to the Dorking coaches, there were those from Horsham, Brighton, Worthing, Bognor and Littlehampton. The Horsham coach, the fastest on the Dorking route to Sussex, was driven by Mr. Robert Whittle, familiarly called "Little Bob," one of the best "whips" on the road. The first stage of the coach was from Horsham to Bear Green, the next to Dorking, the third to Leatherhead, from which place, if I mistake not, it had three more stages to London. The Horsham coach competed somewhat closely with Holden's; the departure and arrival being nearly at the same hour, and the former offering the tempting advantage of performing the journey from Dorking to London in two hours and a half.

In the summer seasons of fifty years ago, there was one Brighton coach up and another down on each day. The Reigate route to Brighton, however, being the direct one, that was the great highway of the coaches to the then rising South Coast town, but now "Queen of watering places," and it is said that at that time as many as fifty Brighton coaches passed through Reigate daily.

There were usually in the summer at the period just named two coaches daily to and from Worthing, but in the winter season one up and one down, on each day. This remark applies also to the Bognor and Littlehampton coaches; the same coach running to both places. At the commencement of the shooting season it was interesting to see how the Sussex coaches were laden with partridges, and a little later on with pheasants and hares. The interest excited then, however, was far outdone as Christmas drew near, by the presence and gleefulness of juvenile travellers going from school to home, and even still more so by the passengers, luggage and presents, under the burden of which the coaches creaked and swayed during the Christmas week. This was the golden season for coachmen, guards, and porters, and too often for coach pilferers, who slyly cut the cords by which the luggage at the back of the coach was suspended, or robbed from the hind boot, much to the mortification of host and guest, the turkey or capon intended for the Christmas table. Pickpockets, too, at that time, freely abounded, and many a poor lady passenger, sitting on an outside seat in the coach "dickey," has found to her dismay on arriving at her destination, her pocket cut, its contents gone and herself without a penny to pay the fare.

Travelling by the old coach had its discomforts as well as its recommendations. True, on fine days and at those seasons when it was neither too cold nor too hot, it was very pleasant. But it was far otherwise to sit outside the coach, even for so short a distance as from Dorking to London, amid a biting frost, a driving snow or a drenching rain. Six hours on the coach under such circumstances, was more than sufficient for one day, but this can hardly be said of having only the same number of hours for business in London. Now, the Rail allows almost twice the period named, in the big city, and takes us in a sheltered carriage at half the fare, and in one-third of the time. These are substantial advantages, but we lose, not without regret, the pleasant pace, the unobstructed view of the country, the sight of the horses, and the hundred and one agreeable incidents besides, associated with travelling in bygone years by the bonny old stage-coach.

THE OLD CRICKETERS.

Surrey has been called the home of cricket, and fifty years ago it was so without dispute. The neighbouring county of Sussex might, at that time, have fairly claimed a similar distinction. The old glory of the two counties has, we fear, since then become somewhat dimmed. Their pre-eminence in the "noble game" is no longer undisputed, for Nottinghamshire in the Midlands, Yorkshire in the North, and Gloucestershire in the West, each gallantly strives for, even if the latter county cannot already claim, the supremacy. The fact, indeed, is becoming more and more apparent that, without the speedy rise of men of mark among the younger players of our county, the pre-eminence so well earned, and so long sustained by Surrey in bygone years, will pass by general consent into other hands. The old reputation of the county was, of course, maintained by the towns and villages severally cultivating their cricketing talent. This led to efficiency, and efficiency to victory. We hear little or nothing now, however, of such triumphs as were gained by the town elevens of the county, fifty years ago. The successes of Godalming, of Dorking, of Mitcham, of Reigate, and of Farnham, then resounded far and wide. The first-named town, in fact, had the proud distinction of beating single-handed the redoubtable All England Eleven. Dorking, it is true, did not attain so high an eminence as this, but it did what very nearly approached it, for it triumphed once and again over Brighton; and Brighton, in the days of the elder Lillywhite, conquered the Imperial Eleven.

Cotmandene, or as it was at that time called, " The Heath," was the spot in Dorking where the old contests took place. The matches occupied two days, and excited the greatest enthusiasm. Devotees of the game from distant places, and hundreds of all classes of persons from the town and miles around, congregated in and near the long booths, erected north and south of the cricketing ground, to witness the match. The ardent interest of the spectators was shared by those of the inhabitants, whose duties kept them unwillingly from witnessing the game, and the state of the score was as eagerly sought as the state of the poll used to be during the progress of a hotly contested election.

The Dorking cricketers included some of the leading tradesmen of the town, and were most of them fine built men. The eleven were taken from the following players: Messrs. Abel, J. Bothwell, S. Bothwell, Colgate, Combes, Drawbridge, H. Jupp (father of the present celebrated cricketer of the same name), W. Jupp, W. Percival, commonly called "Pess," G. Peters, familiarly known as "Ringer Peters," J. Razzell, H. Sawyers, Fred. Wells, and E. Worley. Messrs. Percival and Peters were the usual bowlers, but sometimes Messrs. H. Jupp and Worley would take the ball. The bowling at that period was under, instead of overhanded, as now, and slow, compared with the fast bowling of the present day. Ringer Peters, who was left-handed, was remarkable for his peculiar and effective bowling. His left-handedness, of course, made his bowling a little difficult to deal with, but the difficulty was greatly increased by his extraordinary clever measurement of the ground, and the singular way in which the ball was delivered. These characteristics rendered him an extremely awkward bowler to deal with, and many a batsman who, under ordinary circumstances, well and truly defended his wicket, found his stumps in a horizontal position, soon after a keen-eyed survey of them by the Dorking left-handed bowler. Time after time has the old Dene rung again with the hearty cheers of the spectators at the old bowler's success. The Dorking players excelled also at the wicket, and in the field. This, however, it is hardly necessary to state, for to compete with such formidable antagonists as the Brighton Eleven, required no mean ability in all the departments of the game. It must be confessed that the Dorking players had a special advantage on their own ground, for they well knew how to appropriate its peculiar conformation, while to their competitors the peculiarity referred to was the reverse of advantageous. This circumstance was not unfrequently the cause of complaint, which was all the more bitter when the game went against the opponents of Dorking.

As time went on, the members of the Old Dorking Eleven, from age and other causes, withdrew from the field, but the Junior Eleven continued for some years to maintain the ancient reputation of the town. It is to be regretted, however, that the talent of the old players has not been inherited by the Dorking elevens of more recent years, nor have the victories of the Old Eleven continued to be won.

Very different, of course, are the remarks that apply to the two celebrated cricketers of the day connected with our locality—Messrs. H. Jupp and T. Humphrey—the first-named, a native of Dorking, and the latter an inhabitant of Westcott. Of these gifted players, our neighbourhood may well be proud.

THE OLD CUSTOMS AND ANNIVERSARIES.

NEW YEAR'S DAY.—OLD CHRISTMAS OR TWELFTH DAY.—VALENTINE'S DAY.—SHROVE TUESDAY FOOTBALL.—THE PANCAKE BELL.

New Year's Day was celebrated in Dorking half a century ago much as it is at present. Then, as now, the departure of the old year and the coming in of the new, was observed by different people, in different ways. The Ringers rung "the old year out and the new year in." Generally speaking, the ringing would commence but a short time before midnight, and continue only a brief period after. Sometimes, however, a thorough peal would be begun some hours before twelve, and would last till the new year had come. These performances of the ringers were usually highly creditable, for Dorking at that time possessed a set of ringers equal at least to those of the neighbouring towns; while the juniors who succeeded them attained, under the leadership of Mr. Charles Boxall, a still greater proficiency.

Some in the olden period, danced "the old year out and the new year in," others thought it more becoming to spend the last moments of the old and the earliest of the new year, in meditation and prayer, while of course the majority of the population passed the boundary line of time in unconscious repose. On the new year's morning, and throughout the day there were the same pleasant friendly greetings, and hearty good wishes, as there are now. New Year's gifts too were not forgotten.

Fifty years ago Old Christmas, or Twelfth Day, was more regarded than in the present day. There still lived then some of the sons and daughters of the venerable sires, who saw the alteration of the Old Style, now within a year of a century and a quarter ago. These worthy representatives of the olden time used to say of this change in the Calendar, that they never would believe that their parents went to bed one night and rose the next morning twelve days older than when they had sought their repose. Hence, like the Russians do in the present day, they adhered to the Old Style, thought little or nothing of "New Christmas," and pertinaciously kept the old day, and as they averred the true one. On the last-named, therefore, they regaled themselves and their households with Christmas fare, and those of them who had cattle reserved for the latter, on that day, the best corn and the best hay.

Twelfth Night was at that time, as it is now, the lottery night for twelfth cakes. For two or three weeks previous the growing number of iced and otherwise ornamented cakes in the window of the well-known establishment of Mr. Uwins, in High Street, had been watched by the juveniles with intense interest. The appearance of the "head cake" was the sign that the eventful night was at hand, and with its arrival came also a flutter of excitement which attained its highest pitch when the joyful cry of "prize!" or the depressing one of "blank!" was uttered. Generally speaking, on

Old Christmas Day the last Christmas pudding was eaten, the last Christmas game was played, and after then the holly disappeared till the arrival of another Christmas season.

Valentine's Day was observed by the lads and lasses of forty and fifty years ago with the same merriment and jocularity as now. More was thought at that time, perhaps, as to who might first be seen—and thus be the " Valentine "—in the morning. Then as at present, it need not be said, lovers were delighted when the sweetheart was the happy personage, and on the other hand, much fun ensued, when some one ridiculously inappropriate as a Valentine was first sighted. Valentine letters, too, some of a gratifying character, and others the reverse, were then sent, but not in the numbers they are now. Indulgence in " Valentines " was at that time, in fact, an expensive pastime, both to those who sent, and those who received them, for the cost of purchase and the postage were both higher than in the present day. The postage of a letter from London to Dorking, as already stated, was sixpence, and, of course, from a greater distance, still higher; the charge in each case being paid by the receiver. The postage for Valentine letters posted in the neighbourhood was twopence, and few though they were, compared with the " Valentines " of the present time, a special delivery after the general one was arranged for them.

The doings on Shrove Tuesday in Dorking were quite as lively fifty years ago as at present. In the morning of the day the footballs were carried round the town in the same way as they now are; there was the same collection, too, for broken windows and other damages during the game. How long this old custom had existed before that time I cannot say. When I first remember the morning procession, it consisted of two or three grotesquely dressed men, one of them as now in female attire, and two or three musicians playing a peculiar air, which from its repetition year after year came to be known as " the football tune." Poor " Bill" Smith, at that time and for many years after, carried the balls, with a gravity of bearing that seemed to indicate the performance of a bounden duty. Then there were only two footballs which were usually painted blue, red, black and yellow. The old framework from which the balls were suspended, had not then, as now, the inscription—

" Kick away, both Whig and Tory,
Wind and water 's Dorking's glory;"

but simply the last line, for the former, though commendable for its liberality, is a modern innovation. It was never explained to me why "Wind and water are Dorking's glory," but I have guessed that " wind " refers to the inflation of the ball, and " water" to the duckings at one period indulged in. The Hamblins, poor fellows, John, George, and Henry, or as they were commonly known " Sailor Jack," " Fox," and " Chick," one after the other, for many years, made and mended the balls—the last-named occupation being, at that time, by no means a light one. The game was commenced at the Church gates about the same hour as it is now, and was continued throughout the afternoon. One of the principal tradesmen usually gave the first kick. At that period, it was customary to make one or two bays in West Street, and into these were allowed to flow the blood and refuse from a neighbouring slaughter-house. Into this disgusting fluid the ball was kicked, and the players would go, and the more the latter were bespattered and saturated, the better it was liked. Another objectionable, and even more dangerous practice was then in existence, for in the midst of the game, the cry would be raised, " The Brook," " The Brook!" and thither the footballers would hasten, and while heated by the sport, would duck each other to their heart's content. It is needless to state that the results of this senseless conduct were most disastrous, for many, of course, caught severe colds, which in the case of one or two young men, who had been previously in the bloom of health, ended in a premature death. This deplorable issue had a deterrent effect, and the dangerous practice has now, for many years, been wisely abandoned. Six o'clock was then, as now, the time for closing the game, and punctually, on the arrival of the hour, the sport would cease, and after the players had gathered round the ball as it lay on the ground, and given a hearty hurrah, the pastime was then over for another year.

I must not conclude these recollections of Shrove Tuesday, without referring to the old custom of tolling the pancake bell. The time for tolling was between eleven o'clock and noon, and fifty years ago, the good housewife, with batter and pan and fire all ready, scrupulously awaited the first sound of the bell, and this being heard, the operation of frying the pancakes and fritters was immediately commenced.

THE OLD CUSTOMS AND ANNIVERSARIES.

CANDLEMAS DAY.—ASH WEDNESDAY.—GOOD FRIDAY.—THE FIRST OF APRIL.—MAY DAY.—THE TWENTY-NINTH OF MAY.—GOING TO THE RACES.—BEATING THE BOUNDS.—THE FIFTH OF NOVEMBER.—GOODING DAY.—CHRISTMAS EVE.—CHRISTMAS DAY.—CHRISTMAS-BOXING.—THE CUSTOMS OF THE SEASON.

Candlemas Day was thought more of half a century ago than in these later years. Of the two Candlemases—old and new—Old Candlemas was then the favourite, and the weather on the last named was regarded by people in general as an omen of the continuance or departure of winter. Thus it was commonly said:—

> " If Candlemas day be fair and bright,
> Winter will have another flight.
> If Candlemas day be clouds and rain,
> Winter will not return again."

Candlemas day, too, in the olden time, was the period for dispensing with artificial light, for the days having considerably lengthened, folks then gave the advice:—

> " On Candlemas day, throw candles and candlesticks away ; "

which advice, though having a smack of improvidence in it, might have been taken without much discomfort by our early-resting and early-rising forefathers; but could hardly be adopted without inconvenience by their late-hour-keeping grandchildren and great grandchildren.

Ash Wednesday was but little observed in Dorking fifty years ago, its public celebration being then restricted to the holding of Divine Service, if I mistake not, only once, at the Parish Church. Then, too, the season of Lent generally was not observed as it is now.

On Palm Sunday it was customary to gather willow blossom, or " palm," in honour of the day. It was then a general usage to wear something new on that day.

Good Friday was not then regarded, either as a holy-day or a holiday, as it is at present. On the morning of the day there was Divine Service at the Parish Church, a sermon being preached; but in the afternoon there were prayers only. The members of the Society of Friends, without exception, had their shops open throughout the day till dusk. " Hot-cross" buns were as plentiful and as generally partaken of then as now, and in the early part of the morning the youngsters were as active in carrying out the buns, and selling them, as on Good Fridays of the present time.

Easter at that time, it is needless to say, was a great Church festival. So also was Whitsuntide. On Whit Sunday the first gooseberry pudding was eaten Easter and Whit Mondays were, as already stated, holidays for Club members.

Lady-day, fifty years ago, was of course, as at present, a welcome one for landlords, and when the coffer was low, an equally unwelcome one for tenants. Lady tide, or " Lady-tid," was then, more extensively than now, one of the seasons for hiring in-door farm servants, and on Lady-day the Johns and Marys visited Dorking to buy their clothing for the summer season.

On the first of April, "fools," or "gawks," were made with as much fun then as they are on that day now. Then, however, there was much more practical joking, and more than one poor victim has been sent many a mile through the secret instruction of a letter to "send the fool farther," or has received a sound strapping, when he has gone innocently to the saddler's for a " pen'orth of ' stirrup oil.' "

May-day was observed much more merrily fifty years ago than now. Then, in addition to that favourite of childhood, the May-pole, and that rarer exhibition on May-day, the garland, there was " Jack in the green," surrounded by washed-faced and gaily-decorated sweeps, who, to the sound of hoe and shovel, danced around the whirling " Jack," in their merriest mood. Those were the days when little boys climbed the chimneys, and sometimes when doing so, lost their lives. To these little fellows May-day was a day of real delight, and this they demonstrated by their laughing eyes, and by the gleeful gambols they indulged in. In the early morning was heard the cheery cry, " Please, ma'am, remember the day, the first of May, when I come round with my May-pole," and this was repeated all the morning hours. When noon arrived an interesting sight was seen, for then was gathered, on those sunny May days, beneath the shadow of a row of elms in South Street, a cluster of Maypolers, who, according to an annual custom, disposed of their poles for a penny each. The purchase was made by Mr. W. Norman, at that time proprietor of the grocery establishment opposite the Rotunda. I have seen almost, or quite, fifty children present on these interesting occasions gladly parting with the flowers they had gathered and arranged with so much care, for the small sum named. At that hour, however, the time of Maypoling was over, and as " little things seem great to little minds," even a penny was an acquisition to the money box, and was especially welcome to the little ones, whose familiar cry, " Remember the day," though uttered all the morning long, had brought but little cash to the store.

Half a century ago, and for some years after, it was the custom on the 29th of May, or " Oak apple day," to place a bough of oak in the roof of the old church tower. Then, too, sprigs of oak, with the apple on them, were worn in the hats and caps of boys, and the stigma " shikshak" was tauntingly applied to those who were destitute of the common emblem. Interesting though these customs to commemorate the restoration of the Stuarts were, they may in our days be regarded as " more honoured in the breach than in the observance ; " for, sick and tired of a Dynasty so despotic and so faithless, the nation now happily accords its loyalty to a far worthier Royal House. It may not be uninteresting to state that, in more recent years, there lived at the same time in Dorking a lineal descendant of the Woodreeve Wootton who hid Charles the Second in the oak, and also one of Oliver Cromwell.

Fifty years ago the " Derby Day" was a popular one in Dorking. Going to the races, however, was accomplished in some respects, under different circumstances from what it is now. At that time no railway offered a cheap and rapid transit to the course, and the journey thither had to be undertaken by vehicle or on foot. The " Derby Day" was then on Thursday, and on the morning of that day might be seen a number of carriers' and other vans, decked with green boughs and flowers, and filled to the utmost with gaily-dressed occupants, starting for the course. In addition to these there were the coaches, which for the day were taken from the road, and conveyances also of a lighter description, all similarly laden, and bound for the same destination. An enterprising brewer of the town was accustomed to go to the races with his friends in one of his broad-wheeled waggons, regarding this mode of conveyance as the safest, both on the road and while on the Downs.

The old custom of beating the bounds of the parish, when Ordnance Surveys were not made with such minuteness, and fully detailed maps were not executed as they are now, was a necessary and important one. On some occasions, the vicar accompanied the bound " beaters," who included among them the officers of the parish generally, and a number of juniors, the last named of whom, at different points, were subjected to sundry and divers bumpings, and other operations of a similar nature, to impress upon their memories the exact boundary line. With the same object, at other points, they waded through streams, climbed high banks, and performed other pranks, all, of course, with the greatest glee. "Beating the bounds," in fact, was an undertaking characterised by much fun and frolic, while the interest of the return home was heightened by the sound of fife and drum, and by banners fluttering in the breeze.

St. Swithin was more regarded then as a weather prophet than in the present day. When it rained on St. Swithin's the nuts and apples were, either superstitiously or facetiously, said to be " christened."

Michaelmas day was another hiring day for farm servants, and on that day, as in these later years, the proverbial goose was eaten—of course by those who could obtain the luxury.

The " Fifth of November " is now a quiet day in Dorking, compared with the Guy Fawkes' days of half a century ago. Then the political atmosphere was charged with excitement, and this sometimes found vent on these anniversaries. Effigies of obnoxious political characters were carried round the town during the day, and burnt at night. On some occasions perhaps the offending personage would be a local resident, and his image would be subjected to the same indignities and in the end share the same fate. The resemblance to the original was generally unmistakable, and this added not a little to the merriment which these proceedings evoked. At night, the streets of the town were the scene of unrestrainable lawlessness, and in vain the constables and headboroughs tried to prevent the lighting of the bonfire near the site of the Old Market House, the rolling of lighted tar barrels through the streets, and the letting off of fireworks in an almost unbroken succession. This contest between law and lawlessness, order and disorder, went on from year to year, till at length it was brought to an end by the late Mr. Heathfield Young, who sagaciously drew the bonfire boys from the town, by a liberal gift of faggots and of ale, to the more appropriate region of Cotmandene. Thus ended, it may be hoped, for ever, the " Battle of Dorking"—a real battle of Dorking on the " Fifth of November."

St. Thomas's, or the shortest day, and usually " one of the

dark days before Christmas," was, in bygone years, called also "Gooding day." On this day numbers of poor persons went about "gooding," or asking for alms. Groups of "gooding" women might then be seen calling at the residences of the benevolent well-to-do inhabitants, soliciting their annual dole, some of the recipients of which, I fear, were anything but worthy, while others not only needed, but deserved it. Forty years ago this old custom was restricted to a few of the older inhabitants, and with their passing away it ceased to exist.

The Festival of Christmas, it is needless to remark, was generally observed in Dorking half a century ago, although as was the case with other old anniversaries, differently in some respects from what it is now. Then, as at the present time, the approach of the festive season was indicated by fine exhibitions of beef and other meat in the butchers' shops, by shows of geese and capons at the poulterers, and by piles of pudding and dessert fruits, decorated with holly, in the grocers' windows. The Dorking Town Band, which at that time favourably compared with the bands of the neighbouring places, heralded the season by playing, for some nights previous to Christmas, in front of the residences of the principal inhabitants. Then, too, were heard the waits, the most famous of whom were the "Ditchling singers," who came from their distant home, in Sussex, to sing the carols of Christmas. The leader of these celebrated songsters was the Clerk at the Ditchling Parish Church, in which edifice, even at the present day, the musical part of the service is simply vocal, and where may yet be seen that now almost obsolete instrument, the old wooden pitch pipe ; probably the very same that was used when the old clerk and his fellow-choristers visited the towns of Sussex and Surrey, at the Christmas seasons of fifty years ago. Christmas carols in those bygone years were highly popular, and sheets of them, illustrated by wood cuts, quaint in design and rude in execution, were eagerly purchased. These productions were, no doubt, written by well-meaning persons ; but some of them, it must be admitted, were anything but commendable. Here is the first verse of one of those most frequently sung, and by no means the worst of them :—

> "God bless you, merry gentlemen ;
> Let nothing you dismay :
> Remember, Christ our Saviour
> Was born on Christmas day."

Another carol, however, was far less passable, for its first two verses ran thus :—

> "The first good joy that Mary had,
> It was the joy of one,
> To see her own son Jesus
> Turn water into wine.
>
> "The next good joy that Mary had,
> It was the joy of two,
> To see her own son Jesus,
> To make the lame to go."

Christmas Eve was a time of great merriment and activity, and I am sorry to add of no little intemperance. Then, the elder wine cask was tapped, and this favourite beverage, made hot, was freely supplied to calling friends and neighbours, and to the customers generally of the trading establishments. The coaches, which in the morning and on previous days, had carried to London Christmas boxes of game and poultry for Cockney friends, now brought down distant-dwelling natives, and baskets of cod fish and barrels of oysters, for country cousins, or country customers. In fact, at this time, Christmas presents everywhere abounded, and the poor and needy were by no means forgotten. Then, as now, at the mansions of some of the neighbouring gentry the Christmas bullock was liberally distributed.

Christmas Day was ushered in by the ringing of the church bells and the strains of the band. The tunes of the latter were usually of a sacred character; but I remember the band playing on one or two Christmas mornings, forty or five-and-forty years ago, the tune, "Get up! get up! and put the pudding in the pot," a reminder which some of the housewives of the period, drowsy from overwork, probably needed. Whatever some may have thought of the secular tune referred to, it was certainly in unison with the festive aspect of the season, and not more inappropriate in other respec s than the air, "The girl I left behind me," played by the juvenile fife and drum band on the Christmas mornings of recent years. On Christmas Day there was Divine Service, both morning and afternoon, at the Parish Church, the decorations of the edifice being, as already stated, of the simplest character. There was usually no service on that day at the Independent place of worship, some of the attendants at which went to the Parish Church in the morning. At that period, too, it was customary for some of the congregation of the latter to attend the Sunday evening services of the former. The shops of the members of the Society of Friends, as on Good Friday, were kept open throughout the day, and, it is needless to add, their Meeting House, unless Christmas Day fell on their usual day of meeting, was uniformly closed. The general fare of all classes on Christmas Day was the roast beef of Old England and the proverbial plum pudding; and around the Christmas dinner table was then, as at present, the happy place of family gatherings; although, as in some instances now, the vacant chair would call up cherished memories of departed loved ones.

The day after Christmas, in bygone years, was not as at present, a general holiday; for then the trading establishments were all open, and their assistants, with few exceptions, at work. To the Christmas boxers it was otherwise, for the day to them was a high day and holiday. Then there were no only specially kind inquiries after the health of the household by the postman, the milkman, the waterman, the butcher, the baker, the chimney sweep, and by apprentices generally, but polite calls from, and wishes of "A Merry Christmas and a Happy New Year" by bricklayers, carpenters, plumbers and painters, blacksmiths, whitesmiths, wheelwrights, and I almost forget who besides.

Christmas merry making, and a generous hospitality everywhere prevailed, and social parties were abundantly plentiful. The usual music at such parties then, was not that now popular instrument the piano, but the violin, or, as it was then generally called, the fiddle. At that time, indeed, it was thought to be quite consistent with the social status of the trading, and even of the professional classes, to engage for a party, or simply, for the gratification of the household, the services of the humble fiddler and pipe and tabor player. Two of the most popular of these unpretending musicians were fiddler "Charley" Cleere and piper Hilton, who played such airs as "Auld Lang Syne," "Home, sweet home," "In a cottage near a wood," "The merry Swiss boy," and other old-fashioned tunes. For the fiddler and his companion would be reserved some of the best elder wine, and, perhaps, a piece of the Christmas pudding, or a mince or Christmas pie; of course, to insure "a happy month in the New Year." What became of piper Hilton I know not, but poor Old "Charley's" fiddling career was, I well remember, brought to an end by a painful malady, caused, it was said, by the "weed" he loved so well.

REMARKABLE EVENTS IN BYGONE YEARS.

THE LIFE AND DEATH OF MAJOR PETER LABELLIERE.— HIS BURIAL ON BOX HILL.

When these "Recollections" were commenced, I had an intention to limit them to the state of things and events of from forty to fifty years ago. So many interesting incidents of an earlier date have, however, since come under my notice, that I have thought it well to give them. The history of the singular man, whose name appears at the head of this paper, is so full of interest that it tempts me still further to depart from my original design, by narrating some of the incidents of his career.

Peter Labelliere was of French parentage, but was born in England, whither his mother had come for greater safety, during one of the troubles in France in the early part of the last century. What the special trouble was that led the elder Labelliere to send his wife to our shores for preservation I cannot say; but, from the staunch Protestantism which the son in after life exhibited, the parents were probably Huguenots, and, as such were exposed, at that period of bitter persecution, to great jeopardy; indeed, it is said that the elder Labelliere did not survive the trying ordeal to which he was subjected.

I know nothing of young Labelliere's childhood and youth, but when he reached the age of manhood, he was engaged for a time, it appears, as tutor in a school of 300 pupils in London. While holding this post he succeeded, by kindness, in overcoming the refractoriness of some of the scholars who had been proof against all other means to bring them to good behaviour. In his later years, he sometimes cited this circumstance as an evidence of the superiority of gentleness and kindliness in the treatment of the young. Mr. Timbs, in his *Promenade Round Dorking* states of him that " in early life he fell in love with a lady, who, although he was remarkably handsome in person, eventually rejected his addresses—a circumstance which could not fail to inflict a deep wound on his delicate mind." Mr. Brayley, in his *History of Surrey*, referring to this untoward incident and the mental effects supposed, at least in part, to have resulted from it, remarks, "Yet his eccentricities were harmless, and himself the only sufferer." Whether this rejection of his addresses led him to leave a civil profession for a military one I cannot say, but he ultimately became a Major in the

Marines, and by the title of Major he was known when he came to Dorking. Before coming to our neighbourhood he resided at Chiswick, "whence," says Mr. Timbs, "he frequently walked to London, followed by a tribe of ragged boys, whom he would occasionally harangue, both his pockets being generally filled to an overflow with newspapers and political pamphlets."

Major Labelliere's second place of residence in Dorking was, as is well known, at the cottage called "The Hole in the Wall," a humble habitation, then tenanted by a worthy widow, named Watford, who gained a livelihood for herself and five children as a sempstress, and to whom, no doubt, the additional income derived from letting some of the upper rooms of the cottage to the Major was very acceptable. The humble character of the dwelling in which the latter took up his abode, shows either the limited nature of his resources, or, what would be perfectly harmonious with his generous disposition, a desire on his part to economise, that he might have more extensively the "luxury of doing good." Whatever his other means may have been, it is certain that at this time he was receiving a pension of £100 a year from the Duke of Devonshire, who, it is said, by Mr. Timbs, "had formerly been very fond of his company." That no little esteem for the Major was still felt, is shown by the fact that, up to the very last year of his life, he was annually invited to spend a month at one of his Grace's seats.

The portraits still extant of Major Labelliere by no means confirm the statement that, in his early years, "he was remarkably handsome," for they convey rather an opposite impression. In height, he was beyond the middle stature. His dress, in which he was very negligent, was that of the period—a long blue coat, with gilt buttons, knee breeches, worsted stockings, buckled shoes, and a three cornered black hat. He walked with a stick, and was frequently followed along the streets by a number of children, to whom he gave pence for repeating to him the Lord's Prayer and portions of Holy Scripture. Nor was the religious condition of the children of his landlady disregarded by him, for these he instructed in Christian truths, and exhorted them to the duty of prayer. It was his custom every morning to summon the little ones for this purpose, by rapping the floor boards of his room. The following is a form of devotion which he taught them to repeat:—" O, most tender, loving Father and Friend; Thou, that hearest a humble-hearted prayer for Jesus Christ's sake, save us and the whole race of mankind, as the returning prodigal. Grant that, whether we eat or drink, or whatever we do, we may do it all with a grateful and cheerful heart, to the glory of Thy Holy Name."

When the Major saw in either of the children any sign of ill-humour or disobedience, he would say to him or her, " Come down, proud Jack !" while any exhibition of disagreement among them downstairs would be repressed by his calling out in a military tone, " Order below !" He exemplified a Christian duty also by acts of benevolence, and would give to a poor man, whom he might meet during his perambulations, a coat or a pair of shoes.

Major Labelliere was much given to meditation, and Box Hill was his favourite resort for this purpose, especially on the threatened approach of a thunderstorm. It was on one of his visits to the hill that a serious disaster occurred to him, for, falling down among the underwood, one of his eyes was gouged out. This sad accident, it appears, happened at the favourite spot which he selected for his strange burial, and where it is said—I know not with what truth—that he once had a vision.

I have already spoken of the Major's visits to the Duke of Devonshire. These were made with great punctuality every year on the 6th day of June. The last of these, in the year 1799, instead of extending to only the usual period, was prolonged till September. When he returned to Dorking, on the 6th of the last-named month, he made this remarkable observation to his landlady—" Mrs. Watford, I have been away three months, instead of one, and now I have come back to live and to die with you, for this day nine months (or to-morrow nine months) I shall depart out of this world." Mrs. Watford, who had a habit of recording special incidents, at once made a note of what had been said.

Not long after this, the Major's health began to fail, and, as the time of his predicted departure approached he suffered greatly. The end at last came, and found this Christian man—for such he was, his eccentricities notwithstanding—ready to depart in faith and peace. To use the words of a venerable informant, who saw him die, " He stretched out his arms, then gently folded them, and died like a lamb." Thus departed Major Peter Labelliere, at the age of seventy-four, and, agreeably to a preserved record made by his landlady, on the 7th day of June, 1800,* the very day, or within a day of

* In Brayley's *History of Surrey* it is stated that the Major died on the 6th of the month named.

the time he had predicted, and who, illustrated by his peaceful death the truth of the beautiful lines of the poet Young:—

" The chamber where the good man meets his fate
Is privileged beyond the common walk
Of virtuous life—quite on the verge of Heaven."

Two singular wishes of Major Labelliere had now to be complied with. One of these was, that the youngest son and the youngest daughter of Mrs. Watford should dance upon his coffin. What led to the expression of so strange a wish it is impossible for me positively to say, although it seems likely that this was the mode, odd though it was, that the Major selected to signify that his departure ought to be a cause of rejoicing rather than of sorrow, and that it was fit that the gladness should be expressed in the same manner as the joy of Old Testament worthies sometimes was The act of dancing on the coffin was literally gone through by the little boy, who lived to be an aged man, and who died about four years ago. The little girl, however, having some misgivings as to the propriety of thus doing, sat upon the coffin.

The last-named, as before stated, is now the venerable Mrs. Elizabeth Taylor, the only child of Mrs. Watford now living, the only surviving witness of Major Labelliere's death, and to whom I am indebted for most of the particulars given in this brief memoir. Mrs. Taylor, although eighty-five years old, is in possession of all her faculties; indeed, her sight is so extraordinarily good for so great an age, that she can see to work without spectacles. She says, however, that " if she could see the needle maker, she would tell him to make the needle eyes a little larger."

The other wish of Major Labelliere was the still stranger one, that his body should be buried on Box Hill, with his head downwards; and preparations were now made for carrying it out. It was some time before his death that the Major had chosen the beautiful spot referred to as the place of his burial, and the consent of the proprietor of the hill—Henry Peters, Esquire—had been obtained for the purpose. To meet the requirements of the case, a grave was dug in the shape of a well, its site being close by the seat nearly opposite to an old hawthorn tree to the west of the Swiss Cottage.

One of the diggers of the grave, it appears, was Mr. George Stonestreet, in after years one of the Dorking Patrol.

On the morning of the funeral day, the 11th of June, two carts, one laden with sprigs of box, and the other with those of yew, passed through the town, and all who chose were thus enabled to supply themselves with evergreens for the afternoon's ceremonial. The body of the deceased was conveyed to the hill in a van. The day was fine, and this circumstance, the strange sight they were about to see, and last, but not least, the esteem in which the deceased was held, drew together large numbers of people to witness the interment, which, by the express wish of the deceased, was without religious rites. A considerable portion of the grave was occupied by the sprigs of evergreens which were thrown into it, and the vacant space being now filled in, the remains of this good, but eccentric man were left in their last and solitary resting-place.

Some of the spectators, it appears, did not reach their dwellings without the occurrence of another incident they were equally likely to remember, for Mr. Brayley states that "the slight wooden bridge, which then crossed the Mole, having been removed by some mischievous persons during the ceremony, many were obliged to wade through the river on their return homewards."

Ben Brierly's Journal, after referring to the removal of the bridge, says :—" When the people returned from the hill in the evening they had either to go a long way round or wade the river. Many chose the latter alternative, preferring wet legs and a short cut to a long one with weary ones. Several young men, however, carried their sweethearts across, 'an fine fun there was I'll a warrant ye,' an old lady told us with great animation, adding 'an I was one that was carried across myself.'"

For some years after, it was the custom of numbers of persons to visit the Major's grave on the anniversary of his burial, to have a picnic on the hill on that day, and to engage in the pastime of dancing.

"Numerous," says Mr. Timbs, "were the anecdotes told of his eccentricities. Among these is the following :—To a gentleman with whom he was in habits of intimacy, he presented a parcel, curiously folded and sealed, with a particular injunction not to open it till after his death. This request was strictly complied with, but on opening the packet it was found to contain merely a plain memorandum book." Odd though this act was, it may have been designed to convey to the recipient of the present a suggestion which the donor might have thought was specially needed. That the Major himself was given to making memoranda is certain, for in a little book of daily meditations of his, now in the possession of Mrs. Taylor, the margins are literally covered with writings of this kind; some in a plain hand, others in symbolic characters, but all apparently referring to the events of the day, or the "portion" against which they were placed.

In these jottings, too, there is frequently the name of some anthem, which appears to have been sung by the Major on the day to which it is appended. These sacred compositions, and others of a similar character, he is said to have been extremely fond of singing. He had great reverence for the Divine Name, and so far were his scruples carried, that he would on no account permit the children of his landlady to burn a scrap of paper with the name of God or of Christ upon it. In his later years, the Major appears to have been an abstainer from strong drinks generally, and to have eaten no meat. His favourite food, it is stated, was bread and honey.

Major Labelliere, as may have been already gathered, was an ardent politician, and so strong did he feel once as to the captivity of certain prisoners—probably confined, as many were in his time, for political offences, too frequently for those of only a trivial character—that he addressed a communication to the King, craving for their release, signing the document with his own blood, and telling his Majesty that he would be guilty of the blood of the captives if they perished in prison.

Major Labelliere's piety to God and love of liberty are strikingly set forth in the motto, "*Libertas Deo Duce*"—a motto which was evidently a great favourite with him, for it is found written more than once in the little book of meditations already alluded to, and was embossed on the buttons of his coat, one of which has lately been shown to me.

The Major was the author of several publications, and of numerous unpublished writings. The last-named were deposited in a large mahogany box, which he called "Noah's Ark," and which, I have been told, is still in the possession of some of Mrs. Watford's descendants. I remember hearing, from forty to fifty years ago, that the Major had predicted that "carriages would run without horses." Another of his alleged prognostics is said to have been that, not many generations from the day in which he lived, there would be "awful and generally prevalent wickedness." There can be no doubt that by not a few the Major was viewed somewhat in the character of a seer, while others regarded him as suffering from little or nothing short of mental aberration.

And now for a few remarks on the extraordinary event which has made the name of Labelliere famous. Respecting this, Mr. Brayley says that the Major was interred as described, " In compliance with his oft-repeated wish, in order, as he said, that, as the world was turned topsy-turvy, it was fit that he should be buried so that he might be *right at last.*"

Mr. Timbs makes a statement substantially the same, for he says of the Major that " he was buried in this manner, it being a constant assertion with him that the world was turned topsy-turvy, and therefore at the end he should be right." This is the tradition that has come down to the present day.

Mrs. Taylor, however, strongly questions the correctness of the popular impression as to the Major's motive for being thus buried. She says, in fact, that she does not believe anything of the kind, and thinks it far likelier that, possessed of the same spirit of humility as led (according to tradition) to the crucifixion of the Apostle Peter, with his head downwards, the Major desired to imitate, as to the position of his body in burial, his namesake's example. Such a view of the case, especially from one personally acquainted with the Major's life and death, is, of course, entitled to respect, although it must not be forgotten that the testimony of the writers quoted is clear and positive as to the idea and wish of Major Labelliere, and as to why he desired the latter to be carried into effect.

REMARKABLE EVENTS OF BYGONE YEARS.

The Old Parliamentary Elections—The Mob Rising of 1830—A Deplorale Accident—The Fetcham Murders – Road Improvements—Anecdotes of Smugglers, Burglars, and Horse Stealers—The Great Reform Dinner on Cotmandene—Balloting for the Militia —Proposed Canal—"Burking"—Outbreak of Asiatic Cholera—Emigration to America—Public Flogging— Introduction of the New Poor Law and of the Police—A Hurricane—A Fatal Epidemic of Influenza —The Visits of the Irvingites to Albury—Reception of Captain Wathen—"Crazy" Hicks and his Visits to Dorking—Stephenson's Line—The Introduction of Gas.

The County Parliamentary Elections of fifty years ago were very different, in many respects, from those of the present time. Surrey, at that period, was not divided as now, the franchise was restricted to the freeholders and copyholders, and the electors of the whole of Surrey had to poll at the county town of Guildford. The poll then, too, might be kept open for 14 days, and this was often done at a closely-contested election. It is just about fifty years ago that a contest, of a most severe and expensive character, took place in our county between Messrs. Denison, Palmer, and Sumner. The poll, at this election, was kept open for the lengthened period referred to, and great were the excitement and turmoil which this contest produced. Daily reports were brought to Dorking of the long processions of vehicles, laden with electors, that came from the upper and other parts of the county, to poll at Guildford. Couriers were passing to and fro, night and day, from the head-quarters of the candidates to their various committee-rooms. No expense was spared for the conveyance, or for the entertainment of the " Free and Independents." Official orders were issued for bottles of wine, as if the latter were as costless as water, and band-boxes of favours or " bows," were scattered broadcast in indiscriminate profusion. In fact, the most reckless and extravagant expenditure was everywhere the practice, if not the order of the day; and, at the end, it was said that one of the candidates was well-nigh ruined. Dorking took a spirited part in this exciting contest, and every morning, while it lasted, strings of post-chaises and other conveyances, with the occupants and drivers bedecked with favours, started from, and came through, our town on the way to Guildford, to return again in the evening. Mr. Denison, as already stated, was then the proprietor and occupier of Denbies, and his cause was espoused by his neighbours with much spirit. The Red Lion Hotel was then, as at other elections, his " house," and from its windows floated daily light blue and orange banners, with the mottoes, " Denison and Independence," " Denison and Reform," and similar inscriptions. He and Mr. Palmer were elected, and on the " Chairing Day " at Guildford, Dorking was represented by numbers of its inhabitants to witness, as I well remember doing, the successful candidates, with smiling faces, carried through the High Street of the county town in arch-headed chairs, adorned with evergreens, flowers, and ribbons; to see also the processions of little boys and youths, who, dressed in white. and having caps and scarves of the candidates' colours, shouted alternately to the waving of wands, and, amid the airs of bands of music, the ringing of bells, and the cheers of the multitude, " Hip, hip, hip, hurrah!"

"Denison for ever!" "Hip, hip, hip, hurrah!" "Palmer for ever!" Then was witnessed also the usual scene at the close of the chairing, when the victors, to save themselves from personal violence, had to beat a hasty retreat, and the chairs they had occupied so quietly and so triumphantly were grasped hold of by the populace, and torn immediately to pieces.

Another similarly conducted contest took place in 1830, the candidates this time being Messrs. Denison, Briscoe, and Jolliffe. If I remember aright, the poll was not kept open so long at this election as in the previous one, in consequence of the resignation of the last-named candidate. On this occasion, too, numbers of electors and others went from Dorking to Guildford on the "Chairing Day." The slow ascent of Coast Hill afforded an opportunity for a little pleasantry between the partisans of the rival candidates; and I well remember one poor lady waxing so warm that she gave vent to the uncomplimentary remark that "Only the scum of the earth voted for Briscoe!" The ceremony of chairing was gone through in much the same manner as at the close of the previous contest. The pretty effect of the procession, however, was heightened by the crimson and white banners, and other election emblems of Mr. Briscoe.

The Great Reform Bill of 1832 was now passed, and by it the county was divided into two, Mr. Briscoe becoming a candidate in the Eastern Division, and Mr. Denison in the Western. The other candidates for our Division were Messrs. Leech and Sumner. County elections were now limited to two days, and Dorking and Chertsey, in addition to Guildford, were made polling places. The polling booth in our town was at the foot of Butter Hill, and this was the scene of much animation, not only through the electors of several of the Hundreds of the Division polling here, but in consequence of the sayings and doings of the busy-bodies, called in more recent days, "Election lambs," who unceremoniously thrust sundry and divers bunches of red-herrings and potatoes, tied to the top of sticks, too near to the noses of some of the electors to be at all pleasant. Dorking, on this occasion also, well maintained its reputation for public spirit, and helped materially to place Mr. Denison again at the head of the poll, and to give to him Mr. Leech as a colleague in the representation.

Another spirited electoral contest took place in the year 1835, Messrs. Denison, Perceval and Long being now the candidates. The polling booth this time was erected near the White Horse Hotel. Messrs. Denison and Perceval were elected, but the struggle was so severe that the last-named candidate was not forty votes ahead of Mr. Long.

The only other contested election I shall refer to was that which took place about two years later. Before the occurrence of this contest, the polling places in West Surrey had been still further increased by the addition of Chobham, Epsom, Farnham, and Godalming. This, of course, with the existence of the same franchise, considerably lessened the number of voters at Dorking. The interest of the inhabitants, however, was by no means abated, for on this occasion two of the candidates—Messrs. Denison and Barclay—were local residents. Mr. Long was the other candidate, and though not possessing here the same advantage as to residence, was highly popular, and received from his friends in Dorking a warm-hearted support; and never, perhaps, in any electoral contest were the independence and public spirit of the inhabitants more enthusiastically exhibited. The zeal of Mr. Long's adherents in our neighbourhood indeed appeared to know no bounds, and on the second day of the election, so great were the exertions put forth on his behalf, that, on that day in Dorking, he polled considerably more than his competitor; and as voter after voter came up to the polling place, he was greeted with the warmest applause. Mr. Long, however, failed in the aggregate to obtain a majority, but so close was the contest that, although Mr. Denison still maintained his old supremacy at the poll, he was barely fifty votes ahead of the defeated candidate.

One of the most menacing and stirring events that the oldest inhabitant of Dorking can remember was the mob rising in 1830. A general feeling of restlessness and discontent prevailed at that period among the labouring population, particularly the agricultural portion of it, throughout the country. The existence of this feeling was demonstrated by the incendiarism which was then so alarmingly rife, and by the riotous mob gatherings at that time so common. The professed object of the disaffected was to obtain an increase of wages, and this, considering the wretched remuneration then given for agricultural labour, was, without doubt, a laudable one. The means employed, however, to secure this object were anything but commendable, for, in addition to the tumultuous assemblages referred to, there was a wicked destruction of human food by the wilful burning of farm produce, and, in not a few instances, a wanton demolition of agricultural machinery. The last-named was especially obnoxious to the malcontents, for they regarded its use as the cause of diminished employment and of lower wages. At that time it seemed as if there were something like an organised system of terrorism throughout the kingdom, for threatening letters, bearing the then familiar and dreaded, but, of course, assumed names of "Captain Swing" and "Captain Rock," demanding the destruction of machinery and an increase of wages, were received by agriculturists in all directions. The junior portion of the present generation can hardly realise the alarm and gloomy forebodings which the lighted horizon, the insurrectionary meetings, and the political surging of the period created.

The spirit of disaffection at length unmistakably manifested itself in our neighbourhood, for in the middle of November, in the year named, a mob gathering was announced to be held at Wotton Hatch. The magistrates of the district at once took steps to preserve the peace. A number of special constables were sworn in in Dorking, and these and the ordinary peace officers of our parish proceeded with some of the justices to the place of meeting. From a record which I made at the time in an old "Constable's Expenses Book," I find that 53 "specials"—mostly of the artisan class—were paid two shillings each for their attendance—a remuneration certainly by no means excessive. After a parley between the magistrates and the mob, another and a larger meeting at the Red Lion Hotel, on the 22nd of the month, was resolved upon. Much apprehension was felt as to how the matter would end, and so alarming did the state of affairs become that the justices deemed it necessary to invoke the aid of the Government. An application was, therefore, made for a troop of cavalry to be quartered in the town. This at first mustered fifty sabres, but a threatening state of affairs existing also at Guildford, and an urgent request being made for a military force by the authorities there, the troop was then divided between the two towns. In compliance with the wish of our magistrates, a large hamper of peace officers' staves was sent down from the Home Office. These weapons, were generally painted black with the simple initials and figure "W.R. IV." in yellow upon them, but one now in my possession has the Royal arms in gilt upon it. The magistrates called upon all lovers of order to aid in keeping the peace, and professionals, tradesmen, mechanics and others, came forward (agreeably to a list in the old record already referred to) to the number of 114, to be sworn in as special constables. Of these, it is almost needless to state, only a very few now survive. The officer in command of the cavalry, hearing that a number of pikes were deposited within the precincts of the Church, at once advised their destruction. These formidable weapons were said by some to have been provided at the time of Napoleon's threatened invasion of England. They were, it is certain, used at the funeral of the Duke of Norfolk in 1815, and it is probable were made for the occasion. Acting on the advice alluded to, the authorities sawed up and burnt the handles of the pikes, and temporarily buried the heads of them in the churchyard. The wisdom of these precautionary measures was afterwards apparent.

The morning of the meeting day found bands of the disaffected impressing all the mechanics and others within their reach, and who, but for the threats and compulsion employed, would in all probability never have joined the movement. At last the hour of meeting arrived, but the soldiers—whether from design or otherwise—were absent. They were gone, in fact, for exercise near the Punch Bowl. In front of the Red Lion Hotel was a large mob which grew more and more excited, while within were the magistrates in serious and anxious deliberation. At one time the attempt to conciliate the leaders of the mob appeared likely to succeed, and so hopeful were some of the authorities as to this, that they were preparing to leave the hotel, even if some of them had not already done so. It was now, however, that an untoward incident occurred, for a broomdasher's cart, laden with broom sticks, happened at this crisis to be passing. One of the rioters (it is said a marine-store keeper in the town) snatched a broom stick from the cart, others followed his example, and the whole load was speedily appropriated by the mob. Thus armed, the latter immediately made an attack on the hotel, aud every window within reach was smashed. Large stones were now thrown into the Bench room, and so dangerous was the magistrates' position, that one of them took refuge under a sofa. At this juncture the mob made a rush towards the hotel passage. At its entrance, however, a strong body of constables was posted, and here a desperate struggle ensued. One of the rioters, with a short stake, pointed at both ends, swore that he would " do" for the magistrates, and was already within the passage to effect his purpose, but a severe blow across his knuckles from a constable's staff, sent the ugly weapon to the ground. Notwithstanding the determination evinced by the rioters to reach the Justices' Room, the shorter weapons of the constables, in so confined a space, gave the latter an advantage, and thus the mob was kept at bay. The fight, however, was a severe one, and the blows fell heavily, and in some instances the blood flowed freely. At this critical moment the soldiers were sighted entering the town, and, signalled by the parish constable from the hotel steps, they galloped to the spot. The rioters, awed by their arrival, quickly gave way, and a space in front of the hotel was speedily cleared. The Riot Act, calling upon the mob to disperse, was now read by Mr Alexander Hart. One of the rioters, notwithstanding the warning he had had, refused to retire, and dodged a soldier for some moments round the hotel lamp-post. This was followed by an unpleasant squeeze of the rioter between the horse's haunches and the lamp-post, the loading of the soldier's carbine, and a threat to the foolish fellow that, if not at once off, he would receive something worse. The rioter now exchanging valour for discretion, ignominiously retreated. Protected by the military, the constables were enabled more effectually to arrest the ringleaders of the mob, and in this they were aided by the Chairman of the Bench, the late William Crawford, Esq. The number of those apprehended was soon so great that the coach houses of the hotel had to be used for their reception. One of the mob, it is said, was captured by a powerful soldier, who, while on horseback, grasped hold of the rioter and carried him off in triumph to the prison house. The mob still further cowed by the apprehension of their leaders, began rapidly to disperse. Committal warrants for the captured rioters were now made out, and a number of the more prominent of them, guarded by a strong body of constables, were despatched the same evening, in a van with four post horses, to one of the County gaols. All serious apprehension of a re-assembling of the mob was now at an end; but the town was still agitated by what had happened, and by alarming rumours of further mischief. As measures of precaution therefore, the military paraded the streets during the night, and the town patrol, for a month after, was rendered much stronger. The final issue of this foolish and reprehensible rising was the sentencing of the rioters to terms of imprisonment, varying from a few days to two years.

It must be more than fifty years ago that an extraordinary

and most deplorable accident occurred on the steep hill-side at the north-west of the town. Some fields at the rear of the "Fox" public-house were at that time cultivated by Mr Richard Chitty, of whom I have before spoken, and one day one of his youthful sons and some workmen were engaged in an upper field with a waggon and horses. By some means the vehicle became detached from the horses, and descending the hill with frightful rapidity, it broke through one or two hedges and turned over in the fields below. Mr. Chitty's poor son, who happened to be in the waggon at the time, was killed instantly, and it is needless to say that his death under such shocking circumstances produced a painful sensation throughout the neighbourhood.

About the same time as this catastrophe, another shocking occurrence took place. I refer to the murder of a poor old helpless couple in a lone cottage at Fetcham. This dreadful crime evoked in Dorking and throughout the County an intense feeling of pity and anger, for the victims of it had been murdered, apparently in cold blood, to obtain possession of their little store. A shoemaker's hammer was found close by, and this had evidently been the instrument of this inhuman deed. Three, if not more persons—two of them, a shoemaker and his paramour, both notorious characters— were apprehended upon suspicion, but the evidence was not conclusive against them, and to this day, we believe, the perpetrators of this deed of blood, which produced at the time such a widespread feeling of horror, have never been discovered.

Half a century, or thereabouts, has passed since a road was made which gave to the people of Dorking much gratification. This was the original Denbies coach road, stretching from the mansion to the London turnpike, popularly called for many years after "Denison's New Road." By the construction of this road, and through the liberality of its proprietor, a much prized opportunity of enjoying some of the loveliest views in the neighbourhood was afforded. This, however, was at a time before railways were made through and near "the Garden of Surrey," and before ruthless week-day excursionists, and equally ruthless Sunday Leaguers, robbed gardens of flowers and shrubberies of shrubs, and who, by these and other lawless acts, have done their best or their worst to deprive the order-abiding public of generously-awarded and much valued privileges.

About fifty years ago a great improvement was made in the

parish road at Coast Hill, particularly at that portion of the hill a little to the east of the boundary line of Dorking and Wotton. This spot was then notorious for highway robberies. Indeed, at that time and for some years after, these outrages, especially in the winter season, were alarmingly common. Then, in fact, it was not safe to travel alone on any secluded road. Even the turnpike roads were so infested with highwaymen that about forty years ago a wholesale grocer's waggon in travelling from Horsham to London had to be protected by a man armed with a blunderbuss at the back of the conveyance.

Another road improvement took place about the same time as that at Coast Hill. This was effected by the diversion of the Turnpike in the Holmwood. The old course of the road was east of the present route, for it commenced near the site of North Holmwood Church, and stretched over the hill to the "Nag's Head," an old public-house now utilised as tenements, almost opposite the Norfolk Arms. On the completion of the route the business of the old hostelry was transferred to the inn just named. The old road up the hill was a heavy pull for the horses of the old stage coaches, and many a cold breeze has the traveller had ere he reached the summit that gave him so pleasant a view. The old "Nag's Head" had then stood for many a year, and was not only a house of call for ordinary travellers, but in the olden time in all probability also for those extraordinary ones, the smugglers. Here in all likelihood, these venturesome enterprisers refreshed themselves, before branching off to the bye-roads by which they avoided the town. Such an out-of-the-way house was just the place for them—not that they always shunned publicity, for, as we have already seen, they could be bold enough when they liked. In fact, their familiar knowledge of places and persons all along their routes, led them to travel generally with impunity. Of the "Exciseman" they appeared to have a perfect acquaintance, and to the officer who was zealous in his duties, a great hatred. I have often heard the story of one of the last-named character, to whom they owed a grudge. It so happened that one night, not very far from the old "Nag's Head," the obnoxious official and a band of smugglers were travelling along the same road, but in opposite directions. As they drew near to each other, there was a mutual recognition, but an unpleasant salutation, for the smugglers at once drew their swords, and in the shadows of the night, mistaking the trunk of a tree for their enemy, hacked it unmercifully. Happily for the officer, a gap in the roadside hedge gave him an opportunity to escape, and through it he had crept ere the would-be assassins had vented their rage, but in vain, upon the tree trunk.

Here is another old story—not of smugglers, but of burglars, the scene in this case being a farm-house to the West of Holmwood, and at the foot of the Redlands. Here dwelt a valiant dame, whose ingenuity was well rewarded. One night her house was broken into by thieves, but how was she to cope with them, for it so happened that just then she was almost alone? Hearing the burglars in the room below, and having at hand a store of home-made cheeses, she rolled one after another downstairs, shouting as she did so after this fashion :—" Go it, Jack! Go it, Dick! Go it, Harry!" This stratagem was perfectly successful, for the conscience-smitten rogues, frightened out of their wits by such a reception, immediately fled.

One other adventure in the same neighbourhood—in this instance of horse stealers—remains to be related. Forty years ago the stealing of horses from the Holmwood Common was of frequent occurrence. This led to a determination to stop, if possible, this roguish practice. The stealers were generally gipsies, and one day, about the period named, two of the swarthy race were seen examining with peculiar interest the horses then grazing. The inhabitants who saw this knew too well what was meant by it, and some of them banded together to watch the by-roads leading off the Common. As night fell, each gipsy mounted a horse and rode off towards Red Lane. Unhappily for them, but happily for the owners of the horses, this was the very lane where the strongest of the watchers— Messrs. Buckland and Sims—were posted. The latter allowed the stealers to reach the hiding place, and then rushing forth dealt the rogues such heavy blows as sent them from their seats. A preconcerted signal for help brought some comrade-watchers to the spot, and the robber gipsies were secured, then committed for trial, and afterwards punished—not as horse stealers formerly and too severely were, by the sentence of death, but, nevertheless, by one they richly deserved.

On the 17th of July, 1832, an event occurred in Dorking long to be remembered. This was the Great Reform Dinner on Cotmandene, a festival surpassing in magnitude and interest the imposing celebration of the marriage of the Prince of Wales in 1863.

Long and severe had been the struggle for Parliamentary

Reform, and stormy indeed, in agitation and excitement, were the last years of the Fourth George, and the first of the reign of the "Sailor" King. Then it was that the "Iron Duke," the Hero of Waterloo, was said to have threatened to ride rough-shod over the people, and then, too, was the time, when, for his personal safety, he tried with his own firearms, the bullet-proof shutters of Apsley House. Those were the days also when the "Black List" of sinecurists was published, when the boroughmongers were detested, when, in the House, Brougham, with the might of his eloquence, demanded Reform, and when, out of doors, Hunt, at his mass meetings, vehemently agitated for it. Then, too, it was when Attwood, with his 100,000 Political Unionists, threatened to march on London, and when their rallying cry and that of the country was, "The Bill, the whole Bill, and nothing but the Bill!" Great, at last, was the rejoicing when the triumph was gained and the Bill became law, for then, in every nook and corner of the land there was festivity and gladness.

Dorking shared with the nation generally a hearty gratification, and resolved to express it by an open-air banquet. A Reform Dinner Committee, comprising some of the neighbouring gentry and of the leading inhabitants of the town, was formed, to make and carry out the necessary arrangements. Funds were not wanting to render the celebration worthy of the occasion, and the preparations for it were of the most elaborate description. The spot selected for the occasion was the 'Dene cricketing ground, and here an enclosure was formed, capable of holding the large company of guests who were expected to be present. About 1,200 tickets were issued, and this number, or thereabouts, ultimately sat down to dinner. The tickets were of various colours, and the bearers of them were requested to go to the tables indicated by a flag of the same tint. Around and within the enclosure were banners with the then popular names of Grey, Russell, Brougham, Stanley, Althorp, Durham, and other Reformers. Beneath the fine old clump of lime trees was the victualling depôt, and from their summit floated an immense flag, first of three colours, but to these—to avoid an imitation of the revolutionary tri-colour—a fourth was afterwards added.

The preparations in the way of food were, of course immense. Meat and bread were provided in prodigious quantities. Of water and ale also there was a large supply. The number of plum puddings made for the occasion was extraordinary, for 525, weighing about $2\frac{1}{2}$ lbs. each, were supplied by Mr. Thomas Rose, of West Street, and 60 or 70 by another purveyor in the town. As previously stated the ingredients of the puddings were mixed in large mash tubs. They were then tied up, and thus prepared for cooking. The operation of boiling was as simple as it was ingenious and effective, for the puddings were suspended by strings of different lengths attached to poles stretched across the coppers kindly lent for the occasion. This served the purpose not only of boiling without crushing, but facilitated the conveyance of the puddings to their destination. But of this, more will be said presently. It is needless to say, that the preparations already spoken of involved in design and execution a vast amount of labour. This, however, was contributed with the utmost heartiness and goodwill, for the determination was general that at least for once in their lives the sons and daughters of toil should have a festive and happy day.

The morning dawned auspiciously, and throughout the day the weather was delightfully fine. Business was, as far as possible, suspended, and as the hour for dining approached, the 'Dene was the centre of general attraction. Not the least interesting incident of the day, was the transit of the plum puddings from their cooking places to the food depôt. The mode of their conveyance was a van drawn by post horses, and the cooking contrivance already spoken of was now utilised for another purpose, for the poles from which they were suspended were placed across the van, thus again avoiding pressure and breakage. In this manner the puddings were conveyed from the coppers to their destination amid popular delight, the church bells ringing and the Dorking Band playing. A little mishap occurred on reaching the "Heath," or, as it is now called, Dene Hill, for the strain here, through the steepness of the ascent and the weight of the load, was so great that the traces broke. But this was soon got over, and the puddings not only reached the lime trees, but the table afterwards, yet warm.

In addition to the large number of guests, there was also within the enclosure the band of carvers, including most of the tradesmen, their sons and assistants, who generously assisted in the work of distribution. At the head of one of the tables was the oldest man in the parish, a patriarch of the name of Grout, who had seen almost a hundred summers. The hour for dinner at length arrived, a bugle sounded for silence, grace was said, the carvers fell to work, and the guests to eating. Substantial justice was done both to the meat and plum puddings, and although the provision of them was so liberal, but little remained of either when dinner was over. The afternoon was spent in recreation and enjoyment, and in the evening there was a grand display of fireworks. Thus ended a day characterised by order and good feeling—one of the most pleasant and memorable, in fact, ever spent by the masses in Dorking.

It is now six-and-forty years ago that a considerable stir was made in Dorking, among the young and middle men, by a militia-balloting—a veritable, and not, as of late years, a mere talked-of conscription. The classes included in the ballot were male citizens, generally between the ages of 18 and 45, the exemptions to the "drawings" being those incapacitated by shortness of stature, by bodily infirmities, or by "having more than two children born in wedlock." These exemptions, however, applied absolutely only to those not possessed of £100 after the payment of their just debts. But those owning this sum, although personally incapacitated for service, had, if drawn, to find a substitute. By an old law, a peace-officer who had apprehended a prisoner afterwards convicted and hung at Tyburn, was exempted from militia service (as he was also from sundry other services), and, if we remember rightly, an exemption was claimed on this ground, at the time referred to, by one of the leading tradesmen in the town. A Militia Club was started, to pay for substitutes for those of its members who might be "drawn," and more than one who belonged to it had cause to be thankful for its formation.

About the same period, much interest was excited in the neighbourhood by the rumour of an intended canal from London to Portsmouth, its proposed course being along the Lordships and through the town at the lower end of West Street. A survey of the locality, was, I believe, made, but the project was, from some cause, ultimately abandoned.

In the year 1831, the horrid practice of "burking" shocked and terrified the country. This fiendish crime was first perpetrated in Edinburgh, by two wretches named respectively Burke and Hare—the former giving to it its name—and was afterwards practised by others in London. The crime was committed for the gain it brought, the bodies of the poor victims being sold for £8 and upwards, as "subjects" for dissection. It may excite a melancholy interest to know that the son of one of the London victims afterwards came to reside at Dorking. His mother, Fanny Pigburn, poor woman, had been roughly turned out of doors by her landlord. Two "burkers," Bishop and Williams, who were afterwards convicted and hung, found her and her little son, a child five years old, sitting on a door-step near Shoreditch Church, and offered her a night's lodging. She accepted their invitation, and accompanied them to Nova Scotia Gardens. The preparations for her doom there, however, were not complete, and an appointment was made to meet them again. In the meantime, a shoemaker, then residing in Mill's Court, Curtain Road, afforded her shelter by allowing her and her child to remain with his lodger. On the appointed night, the 8th of October, 1831, the unhappy woman left her temporary home, lured by the promise of a situation. She was about to take the child with her, but the night being wet and dreary, the occupier of the house positively refused to let him go, and it was well indeed for the little fellow that it was so. Had it been otherwise his mother's fate might have been his, for that very night she was cruelly murdered. A month's anxious suspense followed, and then an utterly inadequate allowance was made by the Shoreditch Union for the child's support. The shoemaker, still true to the poor little waif thus cast upon his care, brought him with him, four or five years afterwards, to Dorking. The little boy grew up to be a man, and his generous protector, the shoemaker, Roomes by name, now lives, bowed down with years, in the Falkland Road.

Much alarm was caused in the town in the year 1832 by an outbreak of Asiatic Cholera. A case or two occurred, as I have already remarked, in Ebenezer Cottages, and one or two also in the "Barracks," in Back Lane. So great was the terror of some of the inhabitants near the last named place that they lighted a tar-barrel and fired a gun " to purify the air." One cholera patient, I remember, was treated successfully by the injection of warm water into the veins of the arm.

There was no little interest manifested in Dorking in the spring of 1833 by the emigration to America which then took place. In the previous year some of the inhabitants of our neighbourhood had gone out, and their reports were so favourable that a number of others determined to follow them. Among the emigrants were a few advanced in years, as well as a larger number of young and middle aged persons. Some of them were from Milton, but most of them had lived in Dorking, and the scene on parting with their friends was a touching one, but all of them left their native land amid the hearty good wishes of those who bade them farewell.

It must be forty, or five-and-forty years ago that an occurrence took place not likely to be forgotten. I refer to the public flogging in the High Street of a youth named Martin, who, having been tried for wool stealing in Dorking and found guilty, was sentenced to be thus punished. He was accompanied to the town on the day the sentence was to be carried out by the prison warder, who afterwards inflicted the punishment. About the middle of the day a light spring cart drew up at the Church gates. The culprit was first stripped to the waist, and his arms were then extended and tied to the back of the cart. Crier Chamberlain, in official costume, held the horse's head, and at the word of command the terrible punishment commenced. No sooner had one or two strokes of the " cat " been inflicted, than the wretched youth set up a hideous howl, and shouted in the most frantic manner—

" Oh! Oh! Murder! Mercy! "

The punishment, however, proceeded, and although each stroke appeared to be lightly given, yet the writhing it produced evinced intense suffering. Some of the spectators, moved with pity, called to the Crier to " go faster," but this official appearing to think that his duty was otherwise, went on at the same measured step till the town pump was reached, and here the flogging ceased. The wretched youth, with his back shockingly whealed, and evidently in great pain, was then led to the Wheatsheaf Inn, there, it was said, to endure the added torture of an application of salt to his scored flesh. Thus ended a punishment brutalising as a public spectacle, and evoking more pity for the subject of it than reverence for the majesty of the law—a punishment that few of those who witnessed it would care to see inflicted again.

The application of the provisions of the new Poor Law to our parish, now about forty years ago, created at first much dissatisfaction, especially among the classes pauperised by the old system. Among disinterested persons there was a general feeling that the separation of man and wife in the Union House was a harsh proceeding. Time, however, and a generally judicious administration of the new enactment toned down the hostility which the latter at first evoked.

The introduction of the police into Dorking was from the beginning a more popular procedure. The first officer appointed was P.C. Donaldson, who was stationed in the town for some years, and who won, while here, a general esteem. Great was the regret when, not very long after this excellent officer's removal from Dorking, the news came that he had died from injuries sustained while in the performance of his duty.

It must be forty years ago that a memorable hurricane occurred in the autumn season in Dorking. The gale was so fierce that it was unsafe, from the falling of tiles, slates, and chimney pots, to venture along the streets. Many trees were blown down, and much damage was done besides in the immediate neighbourhood of the town. It was on the Wotton estate, however, that the full force of the hurricane was felt, for here the blast of wind was so terrific that a considerable number of fine old forest trees were felled, as if by the discharge of heavy artillery.

Dorking was visited forty years since by a severe epidemic of influenza, which proved so fatal as to cause a gloom for some weeks to hang over the town. The mortality was greatest among the middle-class inhabitants beyond the meridian of life, and a considerable number of the leading tradesmen and other prominent inhabitants succumbed to this then fatal disease. The epidemic occurred just after a heavy fall of snow, and the setting in of a thaw; and, if I mistake not, it was during, or at the breaking up of the same frost that an avalanche buried some cottages at Lewes.

Many years have sped away since the sight was witnessed of coach loads of the adherents of the Apostolic Catholic, or, as it is better known, the Irvingite Church, passing through our town, on their way to and from the village of Albury. The journey was made weekly from London to the place named on Saturday, and the return one on Monday.

It must be more than forty years ago that an event occurred in Dorking long to be remembered. I refer to a popular reception given to Captain Wathen. This gallant officer had a few years before married the Lady Elizabeth Jane Leslie, or, as she was familiarly called in the neighbourhood, Lady Elizabeth, whose geniality and kindness of disposition deservedly won for her the highest regard. Captain Wathen, just before the reception referred to, had been tried before a court-martial, for alleged disrespect to his superior officer. The charge proved to be utterly groundless, and Captain Wathen was honourably acquitted. I well remember an engraving, designed to illustrate this signal victory, the prominent object of which was a large pair of scales, the gallant officer himself being placed on one side and a budget of

" frivolous charges" on the other; the scale containing the latter being high in the air. The inhabitants of Dorking, warmly sympathising with Captain Wathen, as an ill-treated man, and to show their esteem for his noble lady, determined to give him a cordial reception. The gallant Captain having arrived in a carriage at the western entrance of the town, the horses were at once detached from the vehicle, their places were supplied by men, and by them, headed by the Dorking Band, he was drawn, with every demonstration of welcome and delight, through the town. On reaching Shrub Hill, then the residence of the Countess of Rothes, Captain Wathen with considerable emotion, and amid the renewed cheers of the assembled multitude, returned, in a neat speech, the " sincere thanks of his dear wife and himself" for the kind and hearty reception he had so unexpectedly received.

From forty to fifty years ago, the boys of the period were accustomed at times to be both amused and terrified by the appearance in Dorking of a highly eccentric character, known far and near as " Crazy" Hicks. This singular man in his early days was as sane and acted with as much propriety as people generally. Indeed, there are those still living who remember him as a rationally behaved young man, but an event occurred—it is said a love affair—that gave a new and erratic character to his course, and thenceforward he was known by the appellation I have named—an appellation which was justified by his strange mode of life, and his odd and irrational freaks. His residence, if such it may be called, was a hut beneath a tree by the roadside at Shere. In person he bore no slight resemblance to the portrait of " Bluff King Hal." " Crazy" Hicks' costume, however, was anything but regal. When visiting the town he was usually dressed in a short smock frock, which generally needed a laundress, and sometimes a sempstress. This garment helped to hide others, probably equally soiled and tattered. On his head was an old battered straw hat, with the brim half gone, while in his hand generally was a formidable horsewhip, which served the two-fold purpose of punishing the boys who cried after him, and of guiding and correcting the odd team of animals which he drove in his cart. The latter usually comprised a pony, a donkey, and a dog, each with cropped ears and cropped tail, and to these sometimes would be added a goat, while a cat, similarly mutilated, would, if I remember aright, keep guard in the cart. It was not to be wondered at that so odd a spectacle should

Dorking High Street 1833
(Dorking Museum Collection)

Mill Lane c.1900 (John Walker Collection)

Cape Place (John Walker Collection)

Dorking High Street 1878
(Dorking Museum Collection)

East Entrance to Dorking c.1840
(Dorking Library Collection)

Dorking High Street 1898
(Dorking Museum Collection)

West Street (John Walker Collection)

Dorking Tradesmen's Letterheadings
(A.J. Coombes Collection)

Dorking High Street (John Walker Collection)

"The Bull's Head" by John Beckett
(Dorking Museum Collection)

excite general attention, and that the boys of lesser and larger growth could not resist the temptation of a little bit of fun. The appearance of "Crazy" Hicks, in fact, created among the juveniles no little excitement, and this attained its highest pitch when, with whip in hand, he fiercely yet coolly gave them chase. Woe betide the boy who from want of swiftness of foot, or an accidental slip, fell into the angry man's hands! Poor "Crazy" Hicks has now for many years passed from the scene, yet the remembrance of him and of his odd tricks still remains. It is said of him that, on one of his visits to Dorking, he went to a baker's establishment, and requested the baker to bake an unskinned rabbit, dryly remarking at the time that " it was best thus cooked, as the skin kept the gravy in." The baker, however, fearing the effect of the process on the other viands in his oven, of course politely declined the request. Report states that in the latter years of the poor man's life, he was found up to his neck in water in the middle of a pond, repeating the Lord's Prayer as fast as he could utter it. With these and other painful indications of mental aberration, it is not at all surprising that the closing act of this poor demented man should have been the ending of his earthly existence by his own hand.

Forty years have come and gone since it was first proposed to give to Dorking the advantages of a railway. At the period referred to there were two rival schemes before Parliament—one known as "Rennie's Direct London and Brighton Line;" the other from the Metropolis to the same seaside town being designed by that world-renowned engineer, George Stephenson. The proposed route of the latter was a little east of Dorking, indeed within a stone's throw of the since-constructed Brighton line. The inhabitants of our town and neighbourhood of course took a lively interest in the success of Stephenson's project, and a number of tradesmen and others gave evidence in its favour before the Parliamentary Committee. The struggle between the schemes was very severe, and at one time it was hoped that the favourite project here would be successful. By a majority of one vote only, however, in the House of Lords, was Rennie's line adopted, and Dorking was thus doomed to wait a little longer for the good time then coming. It is not a little remarkable that thirty years after this disappointment a railway—the London, Shoreham, and Brighton line—should have been constructed along the identical route proposed by the great engineer.

Much interest and apprehension were caused by the introduction of gas into Dorking, now forty years or thereabouts ago. Most people hailed the new illuminator with delight, but some had gloomy forebodings of the consequences. Indeed, the latter predicted that the place would be blown up by the dangerous agent. Happily, however, the old town still exists, and long, long may it stand and prosper.

CHARACTERISTICS OF THE OLD INHABITANTS.
Closing Remarks.

The inhabitants of Old Dorking had their strongly marked characteristics. Like their fellow-men of recent days, they were not perfect, but there was much in them to admire and to imitate. The poorer class inhabitants of fifty years ago, would, of course, in education and general intelligence, compare unfavourably with the same class of to-day. This mental condition of the olden time poor, led to those deplorable errors of theirs, of which I have spoken already. Even in their mistaken acts as a class, they exhibited a spirit of independence, though a wrongly directed one, while their kindly disposition in aiding a needy and suffering neighbour was shown as commendably as by the poor of to-day.

The artisan class in general, then as now, had what we somewhat proudly call the true ring of an Englishman, the manliness of a true-born Briton. Of course, among this class, as among that immediately below it, and indeed above it, there were not the advantages now possessed, of improved scholastic teaching, popularised general literature, a cheap newspaper press, to say nothing of those powerful aids to general knowledge, a penny postage, railways, and the other means of intercommunication of recent years.

Mr. Timbs, in his *Promenade Round Dorking*, referring to the business men of the town when he wrote, said of them—" industry and integrity characterise an honourable and respectable class of tradesmen." This description, I believe, was in the main a true one. The tradesmen of that day gloried in their freedom, and most of them could well afford to do so, for their house was their castle, not by a lengthened tenure of occupation, but by the right of proprietorship. Right well indeed they loved, and right manfully they maintained—

" . . . The glorious privilege
Of being independent."

Though somewhat bluff in manner, the old tradesmen in general were civil and obliging. Their hospitality and sociable disposition were at all times apparent. The last-named, however, had its shady results, for at that period, it led in many instances, to a nightly attendance at the convivial club, too often at the expense of home happiness, and personal reputation. Such gatherings, then, in fact, were regarded as indispensable to the exercise of sociality and good fellowship.

The public spirit of the old inhabitants was unmistakable. Fifty years ago, indeed, its possession and exercise were constantly needed. As stated in a previous article, what is now done by law, by rate, by the paid functionary, was then performed patriotically and without remuneration. Thus the old inhabitants watched the town themselves, or, by voluntary contributions, paid others to do it. By subscription, too, they paved and lighted the streets. In turn, also, they served without pay, as peace officers and rate collectors. Nor were they lacking in public spirit in other matters, for they took an active and manful part in public questions, in sympathising with the oppressed, in defending parish and other rights, in promoting the weal of the town.

In these respects, in their public spiritedness in general, in their heartiness in doing what they undertook, they set a noble example, which might well be imitated, more than it is, by the present race of inhabitants. The large landowners around the town, too, might take a hint from the friendly interest in its welfare and institutions, shown by their predecessors in bygone years.

I have recorded with pain, while giving these "Recollections," the languishing and extinction of excellent societies, once so flourishing and useful. Nothing, however, has caused me greater regret than to speak of the decline of our markets; institutions so interwoven with the prosperity of the town. I venture to say again, therefore, that steps should be taken at once to revive our stock and poultry markets, and if a little more vigour can be given to our corn market so much the better.

These desirable objects would, no doubt, be aided by an amalgamated railway station near the town, and another attempt might be made to obtain this boon. Then there are the important matters of town self-government, the restoration of a headship once exercised by the high constable, the management of the town's affairs in general by a board freely chosen from and by the town ratepayers alone; a board, in fact, whose members would be personally, as well as otherwise, interested, in carrying out necessary improvements, effectively and economically.

With our beautiful locality, and its natural salubrity, with our railway and other advantages, there is no reason in the world why the Dorking of to-day and the Dorking of the future, should not stand abreast of the neighbouring towns, in honourable competition, in commercial activity, in continued progress, in increasing prosperity.

My tale is now told; my task almost done. I thank sincerely the friends who have kindly aided me in my undertaking. If what has been written should promote in any way the good of the town I shall be heartily glad. If these "Recollections" have interested the younger inhabitants, if they have gratified the older, and especially the natives of the old place at home or abroad, I am amply rewarded. Blessings, many blessings, on the loved old town!

THE END.